Your place in God's plan

EPHESIANS

by Richard Coekin

thegoodbook

COMPANY

Ephesians For You

If you are reading *Ephesians For You* (see page 96) alongside this Good Book Guide, here is how the studies in this booklet link to the chapters of *Ephesians For You*:

Study One → Ch 1
Study Two → Ch 2
Study Three → Ch 3-4
Study Four → Ch 5–6
Study Five → Ch 7

Study Six → Ch 8-9
Study Seven → Ch 10-11
Study Eight → Ch 12-13

Your place in God's plan
The good book guide to Ephesians
© Richard Coekin/The Good Book Company, 2015.
Series Consultants: Tim Chester, Tim Thornborough,
Anne Woodcock, Carl Laferton

The Good Book Company
Tel (UK): 0333 123 0880
Tel: (US): 866 244 2165
Email (UK): info@thegoodbook.co.uk
Email (US): info@thegoodbook.com

Websites
UK: www.thegoodbook.co.uk
North America: www.thegoodbook.com
Australia: www.thegoodbook.com.au
New Zealand: www.thegoodbook.co.nz

ISBN: 9781910307694

Printed in the Czech Republic

CONTENTS

introduction: good book guides

Every Bible-study group is different—yours may take place in a church building, in a home or in a cafe, on a train, over a leisurely mid-morning coffee or squashed into a 30-minute lunch break. Your group may include new Christians, mature Christians, non-Christians, mums and tots, students, businessmen or teens. That's why we've designed these *Good Book Guides* to be flexible for use in many different situations.

Our aim in each session is to uncover the meaning of a passage, and see how it fits into the "big picture" of the Bible. But that can never be the end. We also need to appropriately apply what we have discovered to our lives. Let's take a look at what is included:

⊕ **Talkabout:** Most groups need to "break the ice" at the beginning of a session, and here's the question that will do that. It's designed to get people talking around a subject that will be covered in the course of the Bible study.

⊕ **Investigate:** The Bible text for each session is broken up into manageable chunks, with questions that aim to help you understand what the passage is about. **The Leader's Guide** contains **guidance for questions**, and sometimes ☑ additional "follow-up" questions.

⊡ **Explore more (optional):** These questions will help you connect what you have learned to other parts of the Bible, so you can begin to fit it all together like a jig-saw; or occasionally look at a part of the passage that's not dealt with in detail in the main study.

➔ **Apply:** As you go through a Bible study, you'll keep coming across **apply** sections. These are questions to get the group discussing what the Bible teaching means in practice for you and your church. ⊡ **Getting personal** is an opportunity for you to think, plan and pray about the changes that you personally may need to make as a result of what you have learned.

⬆ **Pray:** We want to encourage prayer that is rooted in God's word—in line with his concerns, purposes and promises. So each session ends with an opportunity to review the truths and challenges highlighted by the Bible study, and turn them into prayers of request and thanksgiving.

The **Leader's Guide** and introduction provide historical background information, explanations of the Bible texts for each session, ideas for **optional extra** activities, and guidance on how best to help people uncover the truths of God's word.

why study Ephesians?

What is God's plan for this world?

And what is your place, and your church's place, in that plan?

Ephesians is a spectacular letter from the apostle Paul to a group of churches living in a cosmopolitan, commercial, multi-religious setting. And Paul's message to them is this:

God's eternal cosmic plan to unite everything under Christ has been accomplished by Christ's death and resurrection in triumph over satanic powers—and so every local church is a glimpse of our glorious future when we unite under his rule.

Paul encourages these churches that they are like "trophy cabinets" of God's victorious grace. He reassures them that the Lord Jesus is ruler over every power in the world. He urges them to live distinctively in the world and to resist the devil's schemes through standing firm in their gospel convictions.

So as we dig into this letter, written in what is now western Turkey, we will discover precious spiritual treasures for our lives today. These eight studies will deepen our appreciation of God's sovereignty; move us to celebrate God's grace to us; blow our minds with the dimensions of Jesus' love; thrill us with the place of our own church in God's plan, and show us how we can contribute our time and gifts to it; and explain how in our everyday lives and relationships we can please God and show Christ to those around us.

Ephesians will show you God's plan for the world. It will show you your place in that plan. And as it does so, it will radically improve the spiritual health of your church and every ministry within it—including yours.

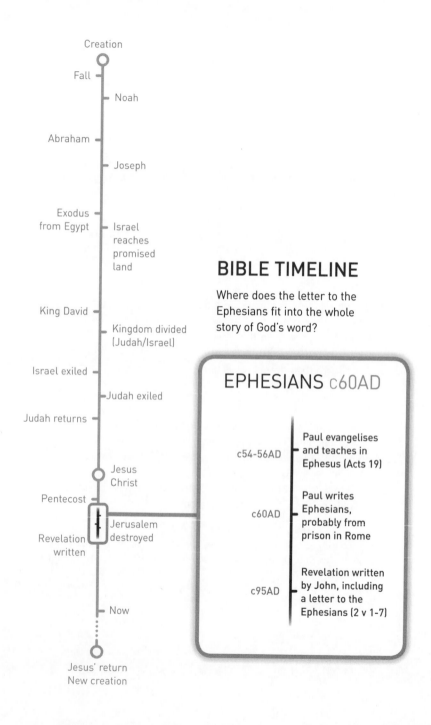

Creation

Fall

Noah

Abraham

Joseph

Exodus from Egypt

Israel reaches promised land

King David

Kingdom divided (Judah/Israel)

Israel exiled

Judah exiled

Judah returns

Jesus Christ

Pentecost

Jerusalem destroyed

Revelation written

Now

Jesus' return New creation

BIBLE TIMELINE

Where does the letter to the Ephesians fit into the whole story of God's word?

EPHESIANS c60AD

c54-56AD — Paul evangelises and teaches in Ephesus (Acts 19)

c60AD — Paul writes Ephesians, probably from prison in Rome

c95AD — Revelation written by John, including a letter to the Ephesians (2 v 1-7)

1

Ephesians 1 v 1-14
EVERY BLESSING IN CHRIST

⊕ **talkabout**

1. What would you say are the three best things about being a Christian?

⊥ **investigate**

▶ **Read Ephesians 1 v 1-2**

2. Who is the letter from, and to? How are the sender and the recipients described?

> **DICTIONARY**
>
> **Apostle (v 1):** a man who had seen the risen Jesus and was chosen by him to teach his word.
> **Grace (v 2):** unmerited kindness and favour.

▶ **Read Ephesians 1 v 3-6**

3. What has God the Father done for every Christian (v 3)?

> **DICTIONARY**
>
> **Heavenly realms (v 3):** the spiritual and eternal dimension, where God and all spiritual powers are dwelling.
> **Holy (v 4):** set apart, without sin.
> **Predestined (v 5):** chose the future for.
> **To sonship (v 5):** as heirs.
> **The One (v 6):** Jesus Christ.

• Why is "every" a stunning word in this verse?

- Where do we find such blessings? (Hint: Notice the repeated phrase in
  v 3, 4, 6.)

If we have a friend who owns an exciting sports car, although we can admire it from a distance, we only really enjoy it when we are racing along the motorway in the car with them. In the same way, Christ shares his privileges with his people—those who by trusting him are united to him—like a king with his subjects, or a husband with his wife. Indeed, Paul says that spiritually we now live "in him" as if he is the air we breathe and the clothes we wear!

Paul spends the rest of the passage (v 4-14) outlining the top three sensational blessings that we enjoy "in Christ". As we understand each, we will be as excited by them as he is. Here is the first…

4. What has God chosen (v 4) his people for; what destination has he given them (v 5)?

In the first-century Greco-Roman world, a slave was sometimes adopted by a wealthy man to become his legal heir, his "son", and inherit the family estate.

5. With this in mind, how do verses 4-5 tell us what an amazing, and privileged, position every Christian enjoys?

Paul is talking about election and predestination, which are often difficult doctrines to understand and accept, far less to think of as a "top blessings". This section helps us with three natural objections to God's election.

6. Work out how each of these verses helps us with each of these objections:

- v 13: God's election undermines evangelism ("God will certainly save his elect, so there's no need for us to bother too much with telling people about Jesus")

- v 4-5: God's election undermines humility ("We're superior—we're the chosen ones")

- v 4, see also Romans 12 v 1: God's election undermines any motivation for holiness ("We don't need to strive to please God because we're already saved, and it's only by his choice, not our actions")

⤷ apply

7. How do the truths of verses 4-5:

- humble us?

- encourage us for the future?

⊡ getting personal

When we arrive in heaven, God will welcome us, and we can imagine him saying: *I am so glad to welcome you into my home at last—for I chose to save you for my Son before I made the world; I sent my Son to die for you on the cross; I arranged history to ensure your birth and steer your life; I brought someone to explain the gospel to you and opened your eyes to recognise Jesus as your Saviour and Lord; I carried you when you were weak and held on to you when you tried to run away; and now, finally, I can welcome you into my home. It is so good to see you—I've loved you for such a very long time!*

How does this make you feel? What difference will the prospect of his divine welcome make to you?

⊌ investigate

The first great blessing Paul has shown us is that **we are chosen for adoption by the Father.** Here is the second…

> **Read Ephesians 1 v 7-10**

8. How does verse 7 explain what we have in Christ?

> **DICTIONARY**
>
> **Redemption (v 7):** freed from slavery through a payment being made.
> **Lavished (v 8):** given in large quantities.
> **Mystery (v 9):** secret.

• How did we get this?

⊡ explore more

optional

> **Read Exodus 12 v 1-13, 28-32; 1 Corinthians 5 v 7**

How do these verses help us to understand how Christ's blood has freed us?

But we are not only redeemed *from* something—the guilt of sin and the fear of its punishment—but *for* something wonderful.

9. Verses 9-10 say that God has revealed the secret of his will and purpose for eternity ("when the times reach their fulfilment").
What is his great plan (v 10)?

- Why is this exciting for those of us who are forgiven through Christ's sacrificial, redemptive death (v 7); and terrifying for anyone who is not forgiven?

So we can sum up the second top blessing as: **we are redeemed by, and for unity under, the Son.** Next, Paul celebrates the third great blessing…

⟩ Read Ephesians 1 v 11-14

10. How is the Holy Spirit described in verses 13-14, and what do these terms mean?

DICTIONARY

In conformity (v 11): in line with.
Seal (v 13): mark of ownership.
Deposit (v 13): an initial payment that guarantees the rest of the money will follow.

11. How do these verses give Christians:
- confidence that they will reach eternal glory with God?

- excitement about that eternal glory with God?

So here is the third wonderful spiritual blessing we enjoy "in Christ": **we are sealed for our inheritance by God's Spirit.**

⊡ apply

12. What repeated phrase in verses 3-14 shows us how to respond to these amazing spiritual blessings (v 3, 6, 12, 14)?

- What other repeated phrase reminds us how amazing God is (v 1, 5, 9, 11)?

13. Share together what blessings mentioned in this passage you personally have been particularly excited by as you've studied it, and why.

⊡ getting personal

Whether you are riding on the highest peaks of joy and success or sinking in the lowest troughs of pain and failure, as a Christian you can always sing: "Praise be to the God and Father of our Lord Jesus Christ, who has blessed us in the heavenly realms with every spiritual blessing in Christ"!

In the coming week, when will you need to make sure you remember this? And how will you?

⊡ pray

Use your answers to Question Thirteen to prompt you to "praise ... the God and Father of our Lord Jesus Christ".

2 PRAYING BIGGER PRAYERS

Ephesians 1 v 15-23

The story so far

Christians have been chosen for adoption by God the Father; redeemed for living in unity under God the Son and sealed for inheritance by God the Spirit.

⊕ talkabout

1. When you pray for Christian friends or family members, what kind of things do you tend to pray about?

↓ investigate

▶ Read Ephesians 1 v 15-23

2. What is Paul doing, and why (v 15-16)?

DICTIONARY
Revelation (v 17): understanding. **Holy people (v 18):** Christians. **Dominion (v 21):** control, or government.

• What is revealing about Paul saying he has "not stopped" doing this?

3. Using your own words, sum up the three things Paul is praying for, each in a single sentence:

• v 17

• v 18

• v 19

4. Who will need to be at work in us if we are to "know God better" (v 17)?

• Think about verses 3-14. Why would we want other Christians to "know God better"?

The word "heart" is used in the Bible not to describe the organ pumping blood around our limbs, but the centre of our physical and spiritual being, combining our intellectual understanding and our personal affections.

5. With this in mind, what is Paul praying for in verse 18?

⊡ **explore more**

optional

❯ **Read Ephesians 3 v 1-6; 6 v 19-20**

Where is Paul? Why, does 3 v 1 suggest?

How would worldly "eyes" see him?

How does Paul see himself? How does he show that the "eyes of his heart" have been enlightened?

6. At the end of verse 18, we might expect Paul to say: "the riches of our glorious inheritance in heaven". What *does* Paul say, and why is this surprising?

• What does this tell us about what brings God joy?

⤳ **apply**

In verse 18, Paul (who is himself in prison as he writes—see 3 v 1; 6 v 19-20) is teaching us to pray not for our circumstances to be altered, but to for our hearts' view of our circumstances to be altered.

7. Why do we find this hard? Why would it be wonderful to be able to see life in this way?

⊡ investigate

8. What else does Paul want the hearts of the Ephesian Christians to "know" (v 19)?

9. How should verse 20 excite us about the kind of power that is at work in and for us?

10. How does Paul assure us in verses 21-23 that nothing can stop us being his "inheritance"?

➔ apply

11. How do our prayers for Christian friends compare with Paul's prayers for his Christian friends? What might this reveal needs to change in us?

12. Write down three prayer requests for others, based on Paul's three prayers in v 17, v 18 and v 19, and then share them with the group.

⊡ getting personal

Don't just pray for your Christian friends to know earthly peace and prosperity, health and happiness. Pray for them to experience the huge spiritual privileges of knowing God better, of knowing the hope to which he's called us, and of knowing the power which he has committed to bringing us home to be with him.

Will you "keep asking" your Father to do these things for the other members of your group? Does anything need to change in your view of prayer or your daily routine to enable you to do this?

⬆ pray

Having shared your answers to Question Twelve, spend time thanking God for each other's faith in the Lord Jesus and love for God's people (v 15), and then pray for one another as people have requested.

3 Ephesians 2
NEW LIFE, NEW PEOPLE

The story so far

Christians have been chosen for adoption by God the Father; redeemed for living in unity under God the Son and sealed for inheritance by God the Spirit.

We can and should pray for each other that we would know God better, appreciate our hope more, and enjoy God's power keeping us safe for ever.

⊕ talkabout

1. How would you define "grace"? Does "God's grace" make any difference to your day-to-day life? If so, what?

⊕ investigate

❯ Read Ephesians 2 v 1-10

2. What three "tyrants" were we, by nature, under the power of (v 2-3)?

> **DICTIONARY**
>
> **Transgressions (v 1, 5):** deliberate wrongdoing.
> **The ruler of the kingdom of the air (v 2):** Satan.
> **Gratifying (v 3):** satisfying.
> **Flesh (v 3):** our natural selves, that instinctively want to sin.
> **Wrath (v 3):** God's fair, consistent and pure anger towards sin.
> **Works (v 8):** things that we do.

• What was the result of this (v 1, 3b)?

3. How do these verses show how desperate humanity's natural state is?

4. "But ... God..." (v 4). Verse 3 is not the end of the story, because God has done something about our plight. What has he done (v 4-6)?

• Why (v 7)?

5. Which words describe God's character (v 4-7)? What does each mean?

6. How are people not saved? How *are* people saved (v 8-9)?

• So what is the wrong response to being saved (v 9)? And the right one (v 10)?

optional

⊡ explore more

> **❯ Read Ezekiel 37 v 1-14**

How is Ezekiel's vision a dramatic visual illustration of what Paul is talking about in Ephesians 2 v 1-10?

How does it reinforce both the desperate situation of humanity, and the amazing power of God?

⊟ apply

7. Think about what would happen to your view of God and of yourself if you lost sight of:

• v 1-3?

• v 4-10?

⊡ getting personal

How amazing is grace to you, honestly? How much of a difference could God's grace make to how you view your:

- God?
- flaws?
- prayers?
- successes?
- disappointments?
- future?

⊙ investigate

▶ **Read Ephesians 2 v 11-22**

8. How does verse 12 describe the Gentiles' desperate state?

9. "But now…" (v 13). What has changed, and how has it changed (v 13-18)?

The Jews used to be able to meet God in the Jerusalem Temple. The Gentiles were excluded.

10. Where does God now dwell (v 21-22)?

• What is this new "temple" constructed upon (v 20)?

⊡ apply

11. How can there be lasting peace between enemies? How is this expressed in your own church?

12. How would you now define "grace" (try to include the truths of v 11-22 in your answer, as well as v 1-10)? What difference will it make in your lives as individuals and as a church?

⊡ getting personal

Is there anyone who Christ died to reconcile you to, who you are not living in unity with? How will the gospel challenge and enable you to seek peace and friendship with them?

⊡ pray

Read through verses 1-3 and then use them as the basis of prayers of confession.

Then read verses 4-9 and use them to praise the God of amazing grace.

Lastly, read verse 10 and pray for help to do the good works God has prepared for you. Pray about ways you are struggling to live his way.

4 Ephesians 3
MYSTERY REVEALED

The story so far

Christians have been chosen for adoption by God the Father; redeemed for living in unity under God the Son and sealed for inheritance by God the Spirit.

We can and should pray for each other that we would know God better, appreciate our hope more, and enjoy God's power keeping us safe for ever.

God has made spiritually dead sinners like us alive in Christ for ever. We are reconciled by his grace; his grace also reconciles us to each other in his church.

⊕ talkabout

1. What is your favourite mystery (either novel, film or "legend")?

- Why do you think we love mysteries, and why do we like discovering the solution?

�↓ investigate

In this passage, Paul explains that there had been a perplexing mystery troubling Israel for centuries, concerning God's salvation plan—a mystery now solved in a most astonishing, unexpected fashion.

▶ Read Ephesians 3 v 1-13

2. What exactly was the mystery made known to Paul (v 3-6)?

• How did Paul know the solution to the mystery (v 3, 5)?

⊡ **explore more**

optional

We are "heirs together"—but what are we "heirs" *to*?

▶ Read Revelation 22 v 1-5

What is wonderful about our inheritance?

How would meditating on being heirs of all this have encouraged Paul in prison (Ephesians 3 v 1), and the Ephesian church in a pagan city?

3. What is Paul's role in the revealing of this mystery (v 7-9)?

4. What amazing truth do we discover about our churches in verses 10-11?

5. So how does Paul, who is in prison (v 1), see his sufferings (v 13)?

• How should the Ephesians see his sufferings (v 13)?

⊃ apply

6. How does this passage change:
• how we feel about meeting as church?

• how we view the prospect of suffering in order to share the gospel message?

⊡ getting personal

Are you discouraged by suffering in some way? How might you share Paul's priorities, and allow them to shape your response to hardships?

⊍ investigate

❯ Read Ephesians 3 v 14-21

In v 14, Paul resumes his letter where he broke off in v 1. He is praying "for this reason"—in light of all the blessings in Christ that we saw in chapter 1; in light of God's great plan laid out in 1 v 10, and unpacked more fully in 3 v 2-13; and in light of God's great grace in bringing us from death to life, and from exclusion from his people into his church, which we saw in chapter 2.

7. What does Paul ask the Father to give the Ephesian Christians (v 16, 18, 20—notice the repeated word)?

8. What does he ask God to do through the power of his Spirit? Try to put Paul's requests into your own words.

• v 16-17

• v 18-19

9. Why can we realistically hope to become more suitable dwelling-places for the perfect Christ; and to truly know the unknowable love of Christ (v 20-21)?

➔ apply

10. How do these verses help us when:

- we don't know what to pray for?

- we begin to think prayer doesn't work?

- we feel inadequate as believers?

- we feel we are unloved or misunderstood?

11. Remember where Paul is as he prays this joyful, hope-filled, ambitious prayer. How does that both encourage and challenge us as we consider our own lives, and prayer lives?

☺ getting personal

I seriously doubt if many of us have ever realised quite how much Jesus Christ loves us. His love is wide—it embraces anyone and everyone who comes to him for mercy. His love is long—he has loved us from before the creation of the world, and will love us into eternity. His love is high—it seats us with him in glory. His love is deep—it took Jesus to the cross as he experienced the hell of his Father's punishment of sin.

Will you pray each day for yourself and a couple of other Christians, for a greater grasp of this love? Why not do it for the rest of your life?!

⬆ pray

In verses 14-19, Paul gives us plenty to pray for! Do so now, and then use the truths of verses 20-21 to praise God.

5 Ephesians 4 v 1-16
HOW CHURCHES GROW

The story so far

We can and should pray for each other that we would know God better, appreciate our hope more, and enjoy God's power keeping us safe for ever.

God has made spiritually dead sinners like us alive in Christ for ever. We are reconciled by his grace; his grace also reconciles us to each other in his church.

Every church is a trophy cabinet, displaying to the spiritual realms God's grace and wisdom in reconciling people of vastly different backgrounds in Christ.

⊕ talkabout

1. How do people think that churches grow? What do you think?

• What might people mean by the phrase "a growing church"?

⬇ investigate

In this passage, Paul explicitly outlines the fundamental principles of how God wants to grow his churches, both numerically and in godliness, in every generation and culture.

These verses mark the beginning of the second half of Ephesians. Chapters 1 – 3 have celebrated God's eternal plan: to gather all things in heaven and on earth together under Christ (chapter 1); through the death and resurrection of Christ, which reconciles us to God and to each other (chapter 2); to manifest his triumphant wisdom to the spiritual realms in his church (chapter 3).

Now, in chapters 4 – 6, Paul is explaining how his readers must live as a church committed to gathering people under Christ. He outlines three basic ingredients for church growth here in 4 v 1-16: maintaining unity; contributing ministry; and growing in maturity.

> **Read Ephesians 4 v 1-6**

2. Think back to the content of chapters 1 – 3. What is "the calling you have received"?

DICTIONARY

Bearing (v 2): being patient.
Body (v 4): the church (see 1 v 23).

• What does verse 1 suggest Paul will be teaching us about in the rest of the letter?

3. What do church members need to put effort into (v 3)?

• What three attitudes does Paul lay out in verse 2, which we need to adopt? Why does each require "effort"?

Obeying Paul's words here really means growing more like Jesus. So, what might it look like?

In our conversations, we could try to humbly enquire after other people's triumphs and troubles before telling them about our own. Before church meetings we could resolve to gently allow others to have the first say and the last word. At our church gatherings, we could try to patiently rejoice in seeing others welcomed and cared for instead of asserting ourselves.

As you look at your own attitude and actions towards your church, how are you encouraged to see humility, gentleness and patience? How could you grow in these areas?

4. How do verses 4-6 underline the special Spirit-given unity we have within our church?

⊡ apply

5. What are the biggest obstacles to this kind of gospel unity in your church?

• How can you, as church members, be fostering unity?

⊕ investigate

> ▶ **Read Ephesians 4 v 7-13**

6. What has each church member been given (v 7)? By whom?

• Given that in verse 11-12 Paul goes on to talk about roles and abilities, what does "grace" mean in verse 7?

The quote from Psalm 68 in verse 8 speaks of the ascended Christ giving his people to the world. So Paul explains that Jesus has not only given to every church the foundational apostles and prophets of the first century (v 11—see 2 v 20). He has also given some people in every church the gifts needed to be "evangelists ... pastors and teachers".

7. What is their job (v 12)? What is the outcome of them doing this (v 12b-13)?

8. How does this undermine the idea that the full-time, paid pastors are there to do "ministry" for the rest of the church to "receive"?

⊡ apply

We are not meant to be consumers of our church, but contributors to our church.

9. Why is it so easy to have a "consumer" mindset? In what ways do you see this in your attitude to your church?

- In what ways are you currently contributing your ministry to your church? How do these verses encourage you in these areas of ministry?

⊡ investigate

▶ Read Ephesians 4 v 14-16

10. What will a church where every member is contributing to the ministry:
- not do (v 14)?

- do (v 15)?

11. How does the image of the church that Paul gives in verse 16 underline all that he's been saying in this passage?

❯ **Read 1 Corinthians 1 v 12-31**

What ideas that you've seen in Ephesians 4 does Paul develop here?

Why does thinking of church as one body with many parts help you not to think too highly of yourself as a church member, or too little?

How far is verse 26 a description of your church, and your own attitude to others in your church?

⤷ **apply**

So the three ingredients for a growing church are: unity, ministry, maturity.

12. What part are you (or could you be) playing as individuals and a group, in:
- keeping and nurturing unity?
- contributing your ministry?
- growing in maturity as you speak truth in love?

⊡ **getting personal**

Do you come to church expecting to be served, or to serve others? Do you see your abilities and talents as being self-developed for your own enjoyment, or Christ-given for your church's growth?

How will you let this passage both excite you and prompt you to sacrificially contribute your gifts as part of your church? What practical changes is the Spirit calling you to make?

⬆ **pray**

Pray for your church leaders, that they would equip your church to serve. And pray about ways in which you are, or are considering, serving.

6

Ephesians 4 v 17 – 5 v 20

CHRISTIANS ARE NOT CHAMELEONS

The story so far

God has made spiritually dead sinners like us alive in Christ for ever. We are reconciled by his grace; his grace also reconciles us to each other in his church.

Every church is a trophy cabinet, displaying to the spiritual realms God's grace and wisdom in reconciling people of vastly different backgrounds in Christ.

God wants to grow his churches as we maintain our unity, contribute our ministry and grow to maturity by speaking gospel truth lovingly to each other.

⊕ talkabout

Chameleons are an amazing species of lizard that can adapt their appearance to match their surroundings in order to stay camouflaged and safe.

1. How might Christians live like spiritual chameleons?

• Why might Christians live like spiritual chameleons?

• How can we tell if *we* are living like spiritual chameleons?

⬇ investigate

❯ Read Ephesians 4 v 17 – 5 v 2

2. What does Paul means by living "as the Gentiles do" (v 17-19)?

DICTIONARY

Gentiles (v 17): here, meaning non-Christians.
Futility (v 17): pointlessness.
Sensuality (v 19): physical pleasure.
True righteousness and holiness (v 24): here, it means always to do right, and always live purely.
Unwholesome (v 29): unhelpful, crass, or rude.
Sealed (v 30): guaranteed as belonging to God (see 1 v 13-14).
Day of redemption (v 30): the day Jesus returns.
Fragrant (5 v 2): here, meaning pleasing.

3. What difference does becoming a Christian make (v 20-24)?

4. What distinctions between "old self" living and "new self" living does Paul highlight in verses 25-32?

5. Who is our great model in living like this (4 v 32 – 5 v 2)?

⮕ apply

6. Why do we tend not to see "Gentiles" in the way Paul does?

- How would thinking more like Paul affect our pursuit of holiness and our desire to evangelise?

7. Choose the two old-self/new-self differences that you think are most challenging in your culture. What would it look like to be chameleons in each area? How can you encourage one another to live Christ-like lives in each area?

🙂 getting personal

What do you need to take off? And what do you need to put on? What changes will that involve?

Ask God to renew your mind and to help you get changed, so that you no longer live like a chameleon, conformed to the culture around you, but as a Christian, conformed to the Christ who died in his love for us.

⊡ investigate

Next, Paul turns to an area in which Christians in the west today are under particularly great pressure to compromise their faith and fit in as chameleons—sexual morality.

> ❯ **Read Ephesians 5 v 1-20**

8. What does it mean to "live a life of love" (v 2)?

9. What does this mean God's holy people must not even indulge a hint of (v 3-4)?

10. How does Paul underline the seriousness of these commands in verses 3-7?

⊡ explore more

> ❯ **Re-read Ephesians 5 v 8-14**

What image does Paul use here to describe the difference that becoming a Christian makes?

What should a Christian do? And not do (v 10-11)?

Why is it loving for a Christian not only to "have nothing to do" with sinful behaviour, but to "expose it" by living differently in an obvious way?

11. What else does Paul tell Christians not to do, and to do (v 18)?

• What are the signs that someone is "filled with the Spirit" (v 19—see also Colossians 3 v 16-17)?

→ apply

12. As a church, how can you more fully obey the words of v 3-4?

• How can you positively seek to love others as Christ did (v 2), rather than as the world does?

⊡ getting personal

Bible-believing Christians often have a reputation for what we deny and reject, but not a matching reputation for gracious generosity towards others...

Could that ever be true of you? How can you live in such a way that people realise that you love them as well as realising that you live distinctively (even when that is unpopular)?

Pray for strength to become like Jesus, who was not only without sin but full of kindness, even towards those that hated him.

⬆ pray

Thank God for making you "light in the Lord", with new, Christlike clothes to wear. Spend time thanking him for the ways you have seen each other putting on their "new self".

Share the kind of occasions when you struggle to live for Christ, and how; and share how you'd like the rest of your group to be asking God to renew and change you. Then spend time praying about these issues.

7 Ephesians 5 v 21 – 6 v 9
AT HOME AND AT WORK

The story so far

Every church is a trophy cabinet, displaying to the spiritual realms God's grace and wisdom in reconciling people of vastly different backgrounds in Christ.

God wants to grow his churches as we maintain our unity, contribute our ministry and grow to maturity by speaking gospel truth lovingly to each other.

We must put off the ways of the world and put on Christ-like attitudes of love, just as Christ loved us. We are not to live in the darkness of sexual immorality or drunkenness but as children of light, filled by the Spirit and thankful to God.

⊕ talkabout

1. What answers would you get if you asked a hundred people:
   - What is the point of marriage?

   - What is the most important aspect of parenting?

   - Why do you go to work?

   - How would you (honestly!) answer each of those for yourself?

⊕ investigate

The introduction and also the summary of this section is verse 21: "Submit to one another out of reverence for Christ". Submit means to arrange yourself under someone's authority. This cannot mean that Christians should all submit to each other (which is impossible). Instead, Paul is going to show us three areas where Christians are, depending on the circumstances, called to submit—and where other Christians are called to lead with authority. Each command comes with a gospel-based explanation and motivation.

> **Read Ephesians 5 v 21-33**

2. Within marriage, what is a wife instructed to do (v 22)?

• What is her model (v 24)? How does this clarify what Paul means (and doesn't mean)?

It is important to make three biblical qualifications at this point:

1. Submission is always conditional upon obedience to God—so if a husband demands his wife disown or disobey Christ, she should not submit to him.

2. Submission is not mindless—it does not mean never holding an opinion or making a point (see Jesus in the Garden of Gethsemane in Mark 14 v 35-36).

3. Submission is not about ability or value—men and women are alike made in the image of God (Genesis 1 v 28). To have a different role does not mean to have a different value (so God does not love pastors more than church members, or CEOs more than cleaners).

3. We might expect a husband to be commanded to "lead" his wife. But what does Paul tell him to do (v 25)?

• What is his model (v 25-27)? How does this clarify what Paul means (and doesn't mean)?

• Why would a wife be able joyfully to submit to a husband who loved and led in this way?

4. What does Paul talk about in verse 31? What does he then say he's talking about in verse 32?!

• How does this help us to avoid making too little, and too much, of a marriage between a man and a woman?

⊡ apply

5. How would your culture react to God's words here about marriage?

• How do these verses help you to view and present God's view on marriage as positive, helpful and wise?

6. How can you, as a church, make sure you celebrate marriage for all that it is, without idolising it as something that it isn't?

🔛 getting personal

Marriage is a vital part of the picture that your church is painting for the spiritual realms and the world around to see—a picture of the union of Christ and his church.

If you are married… how does that excite and equip you to live out your God-given role as a husband or a wife? Does anything need to change?

If you are not married… how does realising that we shall all be joyfully united to Christ alter your view of being single and alter your understanding of Christ's love for you?

⬇ investigate

❯ Read Ephesians 6 v 1-4

7. What are children who are still living at home to do (v 1)?

• What does it mean for adult children to obey verse 2, do you think?

8. What are fathers (and mothers, in support of them or in their place if the father is not present) to do, and not do (v 4)?

→ apply

9. How can parents prioritise bringing their children up "in the training and instruction of the Lord"? How can the church help in this?

↓ investigate

❯ **Read Ephesians 6 v 5-9**

Paul is speaking here to slaves and their masters—but there is much for us to learn from the principles he gives for our workplaces today

10. What should motivate our hard work as employees? What should we not allow to motivate us (v 5-8)?

11. What do bosses need to remember (v 9)?

- How would this shape their treatment of those working under their authority?

⊡ explore more

optional

> **❯ Read Mark 10 v 42-45**

How does Jesus explain the difference between how the world uses authority, and how members of his kingdom use their authority?

⊡ apply

12. How has Paul shown us that we can, as Christians, display God's triumph in saving and changing his people from Monday to Saturday?

- Discuss ways in which you can support each other in these three relationships—marriage, parenting/being parented, and the workplace. Try to be specific and practical.

↑ pray

Use your answers to Question Twelve as the basis for your prayers.

8 Ephesians 6 v 10-24
SPIRITUAL WARFARE

The story so far

God wants to grow his churches as we maintain our unity, contribute our ministry and grow to maturity by speaking gospel truth lovingly to each other.

We must put off the ways of the world and put on Christ-like attitudes of love, just as Christ loved us. We are not to live in the darkness of sexual immorality or drunkenness but as children of light, filled by the Spirit and thankful to God.

We are called to display Christ's triumph and love every day in our marriages, families and workplaces; both in the way we lead and the way we submit.

⊕ talkabout

1. What do you think of when you hear the words "spiritual warfare"?

⊕ investigate

> **Read Ephesians 6 v 10-20**

2. What does Paul tell us to do (v 10)?

3. How does he tell us to do it (v 11)?

DICTIONARY
Rulers, authorities, powers (v 12): spiritual beings. **The day of evil (v 13):** times when Christians are under spiritual attack. **Ambassador (v 20):** representative.

4. Why do we need to do this (v 11-12)?

Paul begins verse 10 "Finally" because far from being a random diversion or disconnected afterthought, this passage is actually the glorious climax to Ephesians—and it is all about spiritual warfare. This is a war that every Christian is in, and needs to stand firm in.

⊡ explore more

optional

> ❯ **Read Revelation 12 v 9, 12; John 8 v 44; 1 Peter 5 v 8**

What do these verses tell us about the devil and his aims?

> ❯ **Read Luke 11 v 14-22; Colossians 2 v 13-15; 1 John 3 v 8**

What do these verses tell us about what Jesus has done to the devil?

> ❯ **Read Revelation 20 v 7-10**

What will one day happen to the devil?

⇥ apply

It is easy to make too little of the devil (as Western society tends to do), or to make too much of him.

5. Which do you find it tempting to do? What about your church? What are the dangers of making this mistake?

- What truths in the first part of this study do you most need to remember as you go about your life?

⊌ investigate

6. What does victory in this spiritual warfare look like (v 13-14)?

⊡ getting personal

How has your view of "spiritual warfare", and your part in it, changed as you have looked at these verses? What difference would it make to your ability to resist temptation if you consciously remembered you are in a spiritual battle each day... who your enemy is... what victory is... and how you can be victorious?

7. Look at the armour we are to "put on" in verses 14-17. It is not a list of actions. So what unites the pieces of kit that Paul identifies?

This is the armour that Jesus himself wore as he resisted the temptations of Satan (Matthew 4 v 1-11), and then utterly defeated him on the cross. Paul here illustrates the armour in terms of a Roman foot-soldier—and it is a description fulfilled in the faith and work of our Lord Jesus.

8. What does it look like to "wear" this armour? Think about how each piece of armour helps us with the various attacks—lies—of the devil.

9. What final piece of "armour" does Paul identify in verse 18? Why is it so powerful (look back to 1 v 19b-22; 3 v 20-21)?

• Why is Paul asking for this kind of prayer (v 19-20)? Why is he particularly in need of prayer for this, given his situation?

⊡ **getting personal**

Identify a way in which, or a time at which, you are regularly tempted, and have sometimes failed to stand firm. What truth (or "armour") are you failing to wear at that point? What would be different if you consciously "wore" it next time?

Whether you stand firm against the devil's lies or not, how does the victory of Christ over Satan at the cross remove your fear and comfort you?

▶ **Read Ephesians 6 v 21-24**

10. Paul uses three words in his final farewell that sum up what we've seen about God throughout the letter. How are these three words great summaries?

• Peace (v 23)

• Love (v 23)

• Grace (v 24)

⊟ **apply**

11. In what way is your praying for the gospel to be preached part of God's great plan for the world?

• How can you encourage each other to pray for others as verses 18-19 lay out, as a group and as a church?

12. How has God's triumphant plan, revealed in Ephesians, to gather everything under the risen Christ as displayed in his churches shaped your view of:

• the purpose of your local church?

• your safety from Satan's attacks?

• the glory of evangelism?

↑ **pray**

Praise God for the peace, love and grace you have received. Share some prayer requests, and for each, identify how Paul's words in Ephesians shows you how and what to pray.

Your place in God's plan
LEADER'S GUIDE

Leader's Guide

INTRODUCTION

Leading a Bible study can be a bit like herding cats—everyone has a different idea of what the passage could be about, and a different line of enquiry that they want to pursue. But a good group leader is more than someone who just referees this kind of discussion. You will want to:

• correctly understand and handle the Bible passage. But also…

• encourage and train the people in your group to do this for themselves. Don't fall into the trap of spoon-feeding people by simply passing on the information in the Leader's Guide. Then…

• make sure that no Bible study is finished without everyone knowing how the passage is relevant for them. What changes do you all need to make in the light of the things you have been learning? And finally…

• encourage the group to turn all that has been learned and discussed into prayer.

Your Bible-study group is unique, and you are likely to know better than anyone the capabilities, backgrounds and circumstances of the people you are leading. That's why we've designed these guides with a number of optional features. If they're a quiet bunch, you might want to spend longer on *talkabout*. If your time is limited, you can choose to skip *explore more*, or get people to look at these questions at home. Can't get enough of Bible study? Well, some studies have optional extra homework projects. As leader, you can adapt and select the material to the needs of your particular group.

So what's in the Leader's Guide? The main thing that this Leader's Guide will help you to do is to understand the major teaching points in the passage you are studying, and how to apply them. As well as guidance for the questions, the Leader's Guide for each session contains the following important sections:

THE BIG IDEA

One or two key sentences will give you the main point of the session. This is what you should be aiming to have fixed in people's minds as they leave the Bible study. And it's the point you need to head back towards when the discussion goes off at a tangent.

SUMMARY

An overview of the passage, including plenty of useful historical background information.

OPTIONAL EXTRA

Usually this is an introductory activity that ties in with the main theme of the Bible study, and is designed to "break the ice" at the beginning of a session. Or it may be a "homework project" that people can tackle during the week.

So let's take a look at the various different features of a Good Book Guide:

⊕ talkabout

Each session kicks off with a discussion question, based on the group's opinions or experiences. It's designed to get people talking and thinking in a general way about the main subject of the Bible study.

⬇ investigate

The first thing you and your group need to know is what the Bible passage is about, which is the purpose of these questions. But watch out—people may come up with answers based on their experiences or teaching they have heard in the past, without referring to the passage at all. It's amazing how often we can get through a Bible study without actually looking at the Bible! If you're stuck for an answer, the Leader's Guide contains guidance for questions. These are the answers to direct your group to. This information isn't meant to be read out to people—ideally, you want them to discover these answers from the Bible for themselves. Sometimes there are optional follow-up questions (see ☑ in guidance for questions) to help you help your group get to the answer.

⬚ explore more

These questions generally point people to other relevant parts of the Bible. They are useful for helping your group to see how the passage fits into the "big picture" of the whole Bible. These sections are OPTIONAL—only use them if you have time. Remember that it's better to finish in good time having really grasped one big thing from the passage, than to try and cram everything in.

➔ apply

We want to encourage you to spend more time working at application—too often, it is simply tacked on at the end. In the Good Book Guides, apply sections are mixed in with the investigate sections of the study. We hope that people will realise that application is not just an optional extra, but rather, the whole purpose of studying the

Bible. We do Bible study so that our lives can be changed by what we hear from God's word. If you skip the application, the Bible study hasn't achieved its purpose.

These questions draw out practical lessons that we can all learn from the Bible passage. You can review what has been learned so far, and think about practical differences that this should make in our churches and our lives. The group gets the opportunity to talk about what they personally have learned.

⊡ getting personal

These can be done at home, but it is well worth allowing a few moments of quiet reflection during the study for each person to think and pray about specific changes they need to make in their own lives. Why not have a time for reporting back at the beginning of the following session, so that everyone can be encouraged and challenged by one another to make application a priority?

⬆ pray

In Acts 4 v 25-30 the first Christians quoted Psalm 2 as they prayed in response to the persecution of the apostles by the Jewish religious leaders. Today however, it's not as common for Christians to base prayers on the truths of God's word as it once was. As a result, our prayers tend to be weak, superficial and self-centred rather than bold, visionary and God-centred.

The prayer section is based on what has been learned from the Bible passage. How different our prayer times would be if we were genuinely responding to what God has said to us through his word.

1

Ephesians 1 v 1-14

EVERY BLESSING IN CHRIST

THE BIG IDEA

In Christ, Christians have been given all spiritual blessings in the heavenly realms, chief of which are being chosen for adoption by the Father, redeemed for living in unity under the Son, and sealed for our inheritance by the Spirit—to which our response is to praise him!

SUMMARY

In this glorious passage, the apostle Paul launches into an avalanche of praise for God. In the original Greek, it's one long, breathless sentence. He begins by summarising what he's so excited about: "Praise be to the God and Father of our Lord Jesus Christ, who has blessed us" (1 v 3). Even though Paul is chained in prison (6 v 20), he feels incredibly blessed—and he wants his Christian readers, then and now, to realise how incredibly privileged we are as well. He summons the praises of our hearts towards God, because God deserves them—and because articulating our blessings helps us to enjoy them all the more.

The privileges that provide such comfort and reassurance to a believer, even in the midst of trials and troubles, are found "in the heavenly realms" (literally "heavenlies"—1 v 3). This is a crucial phrase that Paul repeats five times in Ephesians. The heavenly realms are the spiritual dimension, in which God and all spiritual powers are dwelling. They are not heaven (for evil powers exist in the heavenly realms, but not in heaven), and not earth (for this is not a matter of flesh and blood), and not the future (for we wrestle with our spiritual enemies in the heavenly realms now—6 v 12). The "heavenly realms"

means the spiritual dimension:

(a) where we have already been blessed (1 v 3)

(b) where Jesus has been enthroned for ever over all evil powers (v 20-21)

(c) where we have already been raised to be seated with Christ (2 v 6)

(d) where the victory of Christ over evil powers at the cross is spiritually demonstrated in one church gathering under Christ, displayed in the unity of our earthly church gatherings under his word (3 v 10)

(e) where we need to stand firm against the spiritual assaults of the evil powers by praying for the fearless proclamation of the gospel to all nations (6 v 10-20).

Put simply, we are blessed in the "heavenly realms" through sharing in the resurrection of Christ! The stunning word here is "every" (1 v 3). Each believer has received in Christ every possible spiritual blessing from God. None are being withheld. Christians will have different gifts and different ministries and different circumstances, but we all possess every spiritual blessing in Christ. God has given each Christian everything to enjoy in eternity.

"Spiritual blessings" are benefits that the Holy Spirit applies to our experience of knowing God in the spiritual dimension. And they are found completely and only "in Christ" (v 3). Eleven times in this marvellous sentence that runs from v 3 to v 14, we're reminded of all we have "in Christ" (or "in him" or "through him" or "under him"), by faith in him (v 3, 4, 5, 6, 7, 9, 10, 11, 12, twice in v 13).

We can summarise the apostle Paul's sensational top three blessings under the following headings:

- Being chosen for adoption by the Father (v 4-6)
- Being redeemed for unity by the Son (v 7-10)
- Being sealed for inheritance by the Spirit (v 11-14)

We will never be as excited as Paul is until we properly understand them. So this study unpacks why these are such fabulous blessings—and moves us to understand and appreciate God's grand plan, which he is working out according to his will (v 1, 5, 9, 11), and to praise God for all he has done, is doing and will do (v 3, 6, 12, 14).

OPTIONAL EXTRA

Ask your group each to draw a timeline of their life on a piece of paper, and add to it the four most significant events in their life to date, and then share their timeline with the group.

Then create a large timeline to lay out on a table or on the floor, with the following "stages": Creation; Jesus' life and death; my conversion; today; future. As you go through the study, add the significant events in a Christian's life to the timeline:

- Before creation: Chosen by God
- Jesus' life and death: redeemed and forgiven by God.
- My conversion: Included in Christ; sealed with the deposit of the Spirit
- Future: given inheritance as everything is united under Christ.

These are, in fact, the most significant events in all our lives, if we are in Christ!

GUIDANCE FOR QUESTIONS

1. What would you say are the three best things about being a Christian? There are no right or wrong answers at this

stage. Don't let this discussion continue for too long—you might ask your group members to give their top blessings in a single sentence each. If there is time, contrast Paul's "top three" with your group's "top threes" at the end of the study.

2. Who is the letter from, and to? From Paul, to the church in Ephesus, in modern-day western Turkey (**Note:** The earliest manuscripts don't include the name of Ephesus. Since the letter is general in style, without any reference to local people or issues, it seems likely this was a circular letter written for all the churches planted from Ephesus in the surrounding region.) **How are the sender and the recipients described?** Paul describes himself as "an apostle of Christ Jesus", emphasising that he writes as one of Christ's witnesses, authorised and empowered to proclaim the eternal and cosmic will of God, which we will see proclaimed in Ephesians.

Paul calls his readers "the faithful in Christ Jesus" (Ephesians 1 v 1), because this letter especially celebrates the blessings of being in Christ together.

3. What has God the Father done for every Christian (v 3)? Blessed us.

- **(If your group do not move onto this in answer to the question) What are "spiritual blessings", do you think?** They are benefits that the Holy Spirit applies to our experience of knowing God in the spiritual dimension. So, although we must take up our cross to follow Jesus, ready to suffer for the salvation of others (Mark 8 v 34), we are always at the same time experiencing the blessings of sharing in the resurrection of Christ, and looking forward to an extravagant abundance of joy in arriving home to be with him in the renewed creation.

- **Why is "every" a stunning word in this verse?** Each believer has received every possible spiritual blessing from God. None are being withheld. Christians will have different gifts and different ministries and different circumstances, but we all possess every spiritual blessing. We can safely ignore anyone offering us their special way to extra blessings, because we already have them all in Christ. And we need never feel less blessed or more blessed than another believer. God has given each Christian everything to enjoy in eternity.

- **Where do we find such blessings? (Hint: Notice the repeated phrase in v 3, 4, 6.)** "In Christ" (or "in him" or "through him" or "under him"), by faith in him (v 3, 4, 5, 6, 7, 9, 10, 11, 12, twice in v 13). God wants us to remember that we owe everything to his Son. We're blessed not just "through" Christ, as the mechanism for getting blessed, but personally "in" Christ, to whom we are united by faith. These are his fabulous resurrection blessings, and we enjoy them if we have turned to trust in him.

4. What has God chosen (v 4) his people for; what destination has he given them (v 5)? For "adoption". He has predestined us (ie: fixed our destination) to be his children, part of his family, eternally.

5. With this in mind, how do verses 4-5 tell us what an amazing, and privileged, position every Christian enjoys? By faith in God's Son, men and women alike are adopted by the Father to share in Jesus' inheritance. He has chosen to unite us

with his Son, by faith, to enjoy his Son's privileges. We enjoy the tender love of our heavenly Father, carefully providing our daily needs, pardoning our sins, protecting us from harm, disciplining us in the way we should go, and showering us with undeserved kindnesses. We enjoy our heavenly Father's constant attention to our prayers, for he's never sleepy or forgetful, never grumpy or uninterested, never powerless to help or unsure of what to do. Indeed, in Christ we are brought right into the family of the triune God himself, able to whisper in the ear of our Father!
Note: To draw all this out, you may need to ask: What kind of things will God do for us as our Father?

6. Work out how each of these verses helps us with each of these objections:

- **v 13: God's election undermines evangelism ("God will certainly save his elect, so there's no need for us to bother too much with telling people about Jesus")** It is through the preaching of the gospel of Christ that God calls his elect into Christ, as they hear the message of salvation. God uses our evangelism to save his elect. Indeed, if God hadn't elected anyone for us to call to him through the gospel, there would be no point in us trying to evangelise sinners because they're spiritually dead (2:1). But since God has elected many, we evangelise everyone, in the confidence that he can involve us in reaching his elect! Election motivates evangelism.

- **v 4-5: God's election undermines humility ("We're superior—we're the chosen ones")** We're not saved because we turned out to be cleverer or more deserving than other people. The decision was made long before we were even born—before God even created the world. Being "chosen" should humble us by reminding us that we're not more deserving than our atheist or Muslim friends. If we had chosen God without him first choosing us, then we could be proud of our wisdom. Since he first chose us, we should only ever be humble—our salvation was entirely due to his gracious initiative.

• **v 4, see also Romans 12 v 1: God's election undermines any motivation for holiness ("We don't need to strive to please God because we're already saved, and it's only by his choice, not our actions")** We've been chosen to be accepted by God as holy and blameless on the basis of the holy and blameless life lived for us by Jesus. And then, in gratitude for being saved (see Romans 12 v 1), we're called to gradually become holy and blameless like him. Because we've been chosen to play for the highly privileged "Holy and Blameless Team", captained by Jesus, we will want to become holy and blameless like him. Election is a reason to be holy!

7. APPLY: How do the truths of v 4-5:
• **humble us?** We did not choose God; he chose us. And he chose us because of his love for us, not because of our work for him. All we have is given to us, not earned by us. This is deeply humbling.

• **encourage us for the future?** If we are "in Christ", we have confidence for the future. God has not left any part of his plan uncertain or risky. All that happens will always happen according to his "will" (see also v 10). It's precisely because our God has planned everything and has everything under control that Christians can relax and not worry about the things we don't know and can't control. There

is a certain and glorious future awaiting believers, even as we struggle now with personal failures and addictions, or debilitating physical and mental conditions, or miserable jobs or unemployment, or painful singleness, divorce or widowhood. Whatever we face, Christians can be sure that we are children of God now, and will be in eternal glory with him in 200 years' time (and probably sooner!).

8. How does verse 7 explain what we have in Christ? Redemption—liberation from slavery, to enjoy being free, having had our sins forgiven (we will see more of this in Study Three when we reach 2 v 1-3).

• **How did we get this?** Through his blood. It is Christ's death that liberates us.

EXPLORE MORE
Read Exodus 12 v 1-13, 28-32; 1 Corinthians 5 v 7. How do these verses help us to understand how Christ's blood has freed us? The Passover lambs were sacrificed in the place of the Israelite firstborn sons, suffering the punishment that Israel deserved (the death of all their firstborn), and their blood was then painted over the doorposts of Israelite houses. When God saw that the death penalty for sin had already occurred, his judgment "passed over" the Israelites. It is similar now for Christians. Jesus is our "Passover" sacrifice (1 Cor 5 v 7). His death is as a sacrificial Passover lamb, suffering God's wrath against our sin on the cross. We trust in his precious blood—and so the death penalty for our sins has already occurred.

9. Verses 9-10 say that God has revealed the secret of his will and purpose for eternity ("when the times reach their fulfilment"). What is his great plan

(v 10)? "To bring unity to all things in heaven and on earth under Christ". God's plan is to bring together (literally, to "sum up") everything under Christ, including rebellious evil spirits in the heavenly realms and rebellious human beings on the earth. Everything will be re-ordered in appropriate submission to God.

Note: This is not undermining Jesus' clear and frightening teaching that after death, unrepentant sinners and demons will be condemned to hell (eg: Matthew 25:41). Paul is simply explaining that God's just order will be fully restored everywhere, under the rule of Christ.

- **Why is this exciting for those of us who are forgiven through Christ's sacrificial, redemptive death (v 7); and terrifying for anyone who is not forgiven?** We know where we are headed—and we know where everything is headed. If we are "in Christ", we are on the right side of history. The one who rules, and who will rule everything for ever, is the one who loves us, and has died for us so that we can be his subjects, enjoying life with him. The divine Architect has published his glorious construction plan, and, having laid the sure foundation in the death and resurrection of Christ, the completion of his glorious new creation is now just a matter of time.

  But for anyone who is not in Christ, the prospect of meeting him as their King and Judge, having spent their lives rebelling against him, should be horrifying—and bring them to repentance (Acts 2 v 38-41).

10. How is the Holy Spirit described in v 13-14, and what do these terms mean?
- A "seal" (v 13): A "seal" was a mark of ownership and protection, which in Roman culture was often branded upon

cattle or slaves. God's seal of permanent ownership and constant protection of his people is the Holy Spirit of God himself. He is therefore like the birthmark of all God's children. It is as though we have all been marked with a spiritual UV marker pen, visible in the heavenly realms, marking us out as those belonging to God, completely safe from all frightening powers.
- A "deposit" (v 14): the first instalment of eternal life, guaranteeing the "full payment" of enjoying God in heaven, because he is God within us. He is like the delicious first course of the spiritual feast to come in the new creation.

11. How do these verses give Christians:
- **confidence that they will reach eternal glory with God?** God has marked us as his own—and he is in charge of the future. There is no doubt in the spiritual realms that we belong to God, as his children. If reaching eternal glory was up to us, we would have great cause for worry and uncertainty. But it is up to God—and he has put his Spirit in us as a "seal"—the sign that we are his.

- **excitement about that eternal glory with God?** Knowing that the Spirit is "merely" a deposit means we'll avoid thinking that our current experience as Christians is all there is or the best there is, when it is actually only the deposit—a taste of what is yet to come! The Holy Spirit's ministry in us now is a mouth-watering foretaste of the feast we shall enjoy in the presence of God.

12. APPLY: What repeated phrase in verses 3-14 shows us how to respond to these amazing spiritual blessings (v 3, 6, 12, 14)? God's blessings in our lives are intended to be "to the praise of his glory". These wonderful privileges are meant to stir our hearts to serve him with the worship of our whole lives, and to open our mouths to praise him in adoration and evangelism. When we're feeling sorry for ourselves, or going through difficult times, or being persecuted for our faith in Christ, we can return to this glorious passage to be reminded of how extravagantly blessed we are in knowing Christ.

• **What other repeated phrase reminds us how amazing God is (v 1, 5, 9, 11)?** These blessings have been granted according to God's will. Paul wants his readers to remember and rejoice about the truth that God is accomplishing his grand plan—the history of the world is not random. We're not accidents, and our lives are not pointless. Everything is being executed by God exactly according to his will and purpose, so there's no need to be anxious when things "go wrong", and every reason to praise him instead.

13. APPLY: Share together what blessings mentioned in this passage you personally have been particularly excited by as you've studied it, and why. Give time to allow your group to encourage each other as they share the different ways these blessings have excited them in their differing life circumstances. Make sure you focus on the blessings Paul does here in this passage!

Ephesians 1 v 15-23
2 PRAYING BIGGER PRAYERS

THE BIG IDEA
We can and should pray for our Christian friends, and pray that they would know God better, appreciate more the hope they have more, and enjoy God's power working in their lives.

SUMMARY
In another extraordinary passage, Paul reveals to the Ephesian churches what he's been praying for them. As in most of his letters, he's providing warm reassurance of his affection for them and explaining what he thinks they most need from God. But when we compare the content of his prayer with our own praying, we'll probably be astonished by how seriously theological Paul's is! It doesn't contain any requests for material blessings like better health or jobs;

or for relational blessings at work, or for marriages or in raising children. It's a prayer for deep spiritual blessings in knowing God. As we explore Paul's prayer points, we'll be learning a lot about how to pray. We'll see that we can (and ought to) pray for our Christian friends and family members to:
• know God better (v 17)
• appreciate our future hope more, and "see" our lives in light of it (v 18)
• remember God's resurrection power is and will be at work in us (v 19).

Since this study focuses on prayer, ensure you move through quickly enough to leave lots of time to pray at the end of your time.

OPTIONAL EXTRA
Before you meet, ask group members

to read a book (or section of a book) on praying, or collections of prayers: for instance, *Of Prayer* (John Calvin); *Prayer: Experiencing Intimacy and Awe with God* (Tim Keller); *A Praying Life* (Paul Miller); *The Valley of Vision* (ed Arthur Bennett). As them to share a few things that struck them and helped them in their own prayers. You could do this at the start or end of the session.

GUIDANCE FOR QUESTIONS

1. When you pray for Christian friends or family members, what kind of things do you tend to pray about? The aim of this is to help your group think not just about whether they pray for others, but what they pray for them. We tend to ask for material blessings (better health, new job, etc.) or relational blessings (marriage, help with raising children, etc.). Tell the group that in this session, they'll see Paul praying for his Christian friends—and will probably be astonished at how seriously theological it is! As you explore Paul's prayer points, you'll be learning a lot about how to pray.

2. What is Paul doing, and why (v 15-16)? He is "giving thanks for" the Ephesian Christians—for their faith in God and their love for each other; and he is doing so "for this reason" (v 15), meaning: *Because of what I've just said in v 1-14 about God gathering his chosen, redeemed and sealed people, I give thanks for your faith.*

• **What is revealing about Paul saying he has "not stopped" doing this?** Paul prayed unceasingly—regularly. Prayer was a constant feature of his life. He was usually ferociously busy and was now suffering in prison; but he still prayed for his Christian friends all the time. He could have stopped praying (too busy, or too

struggling); or simply prayed for himself, for his busyness and struggles. But he did not.

3. Using your own words, sum up the three things Paul is praying for, each in a single sentence: (Obviously, as your group use their own words they will not come up with exactly these answers!)

• **v 17:** That they will know God better, through his Spirit's work in them.

• **v 18:** That their hearts will be more and more dominated and directed by the great hope they have in Christ.

• **v 19:** That they will appreciate the immense power of God that works in them to secure them in faith and for their future.

4. Who will need to be at work in us if we are to "know God better" (v 17)? His Spirit—the Spirit of "wisdom and revelation", who will bring a deeper understanding of God as he is revealed in his Spirit-inspired word, so that we can get to know him better and better.

• **Think about verses 3-14. Why would we want other Christians to "know God better"?** Because he is our creating, ruling, electing, redeeming, sealing, glorifying God, who loves us. It is wonderful to know well someone who loves you. In a good marriage, one of the greatest joys is simply coming to know the other person more and more, and so to appreciate them more and more. God is perfect—the more we know him, the more we will know his love for us and enjoy loving him.

5. With this in mind [ie: that heart is used in the Bible to described the centre of our being], what is Paul praying for

in verse 18? That we will be able to "see" the world in an "enlightened" way—a Christ-centred way—that we will love the things God loves, and trust God to be at work, so that we are confident that no matter what happens we are headed for our inheritance in heaven.

EXPLORE MORE
Read Ephesians 3 v 1; 6 v 19-20. Where is Paul? Why, does 3 v 1 suggest? He is a prisoner, because of his faithful witness to Christ.
How would worldly "eyes" see him? As a defeated, failed preacher, trapped in prison.
How does Paul see himself? As an ambassador of Christ, displaying his glory to others and sharing his gospel with them. **How does he show the "eyes of his heart" have been enlightened?** His perspective is not dominated by his circumstances, but by his Saviour, so that prison becomes an opportunity to share Christ with the other prisoners and the guards.

6. At the end of v 18, we might expect Paul to say: "the riches of our glorious inheritance in heaven". What does Paul say, and why is this surprising? Paul talks about "the riches of his glorious inheritance in his holy people". He's talking about us—God has saved sinners to be "his inheritance". He will welcome us with open arms, as the most precious thing in his new creation.

• **What does this tell us about what brings God joy?** We do! God will enjoy our company and shower us with abundant blessings for ever.

7. APPLY: Why do we find [praying

for our hearts' view rather than our circumstances to be altered] hard? Because the world lives by sight, not by faith—and so do we, naturally. We tend to think that our success as people rests in how good our circumstances are, and that changing our circumstances is what will bring us the things we want in life—satisfaction, security, and so on. Often, in how we speak to one another and pray for one another, we reinforce this to one another. **Why would it be wonderful to be able to see life in this way?** Because if we see life in a way that always remembers that Christ is reigning on high, and that we are on our way home, then we don't need to escape from our reality, or to seek to change our reality at any cost. We can be confident and not fearful, however great our flaws or problems.

8. What else does Paul want the hearts of the Ephesian Christians to "know" (v 19)? "His incomparably great power" for believers.

9. How should verse 20 excite us about the kind of power that is at work in and for us? It is a power great enough to raise Jesus from the dead and seat him in the heavenly realms. That same power is now used to keep us going in faith, and will be used to raise us too. We could say that God has practised resurrecting us in raising Jesus. He's done it before, so we know he can do it again.

10. How does Paul assure us in verses 21-23 that nothing can stop us being his "inheritance"? Our Saviour is enthroned far above all evil powers—above every position imaginable. And he rules "for" (ie: for the benefit of) his church (v 22). However small our churches or however vulnerable we feel, all God's resurrection power is being used to keep churches trusting Christ. There is no one more powerful than our Lord.

11. APPLY: How do our prayers for Christian friends compare with Paul's prayers for his Christian friends? What might this reveal needs to change in us? You could refer back to Q1 here. Make clear that we are not only to pray what Paul does in Ephesians 1. But we should at least be praying these things for our friends, and praying them regularly.

⊻

• **Why do you think our prayers are less bold and less God-focused than Paul's?**

12. APPLY: Write down three prayer requests for others, based on Paul's three prayers in v 17, v 18 and v 19, and then share them with the group. Encourage your group to write down others' prayer requests, or gather them in yourself to email round afterwards. Then spend time at the end using these as the basis for your prayers—and also challenge your group members to pray for each other using the themes of the passage in the coming week (and beyond).

3 Ephesians 2
NEW LIFE, NEW PEOPLE

THE BIG IDEA
By God's grace in Christ's life, death and resurrection, we have been reconciled to God and given eternal life; and we have been reconciled to each other and are being built into his church.

SUMMARY
In this wonderful section, Paul explains how we have been reconciled to God through Christ; and how we have been reconciled to each other by God through Christ. Fundamentally, this whole passage is about the transforming nature of God's grace. By grace, he gives us faith in Christ, and so brings us from spiritual death, facing his wrath, to spiritual life, seated in heaven with Christ, and with eternity with him to look forward to. And by grace, he brings us into

his church, in which he dwells, abolishing all that divides us as humans—even the divide between Jew and Gentile.

So in this study, you will see the desperate state of those who live in rebellion against God (by nature, all of us), and of those who live outside God's people (in the Old Testament, the "Gentiles"). And you will see the wonderful new humanity created by God, by bringing dead rebels to life and bringing Jews and Gentiles into his people through the cross.

OPTIONAL EXTRA
Ask one or two people briefly to summarise the story of how they became a Christian. Set a timer for a minute and challenge them to tell their story within the time limit! Ask them to base it on four points:

- How I saw my non-Christian life before I became Christian.
- How I came to see that life when I became a Christian.
- Why I became a Christian.
- How my outlook and life is different now.

GUIDANCE FOR QUESTIONS

1. How would you define "grace"? Does "God's grace" make any difference to your day-to-day life? If so, what? If your group spend a while discussing the first part of this question, then skip the second part. But if your group are already clear on what grace is, then spend longer on the second part. If we have been in Bible-teaching churches for a while, we probably have a good explanation of what grace is—but that does not mean it actually makes much difference to our lives.

2. What three "tyrants" were we, by nature, under the power of (v 2-3)?

1. "The ways of this world"—an external cultural tyranny. We follow a cultural worldview of our sinful race. At present, there are two principal worldviews across the globe: first, a "traditional" one, concerned with social hierarchy, duty, and good works, which rejects the gospel because it does not see a need for a Saviour, since good works and dutiful living are enough. Second, the "emergent" worldview, which is self-focused, pluralistic and/or atheistic, and that worships idols such as sex, pleasure, power, family, etc. It rejects the gospel because it does not recognise Jesus as Lord.

2. "The ruler of the kingdom of the air"— the devil, a hostile supernatural tyranny. In Hebrew thinking, Satan exists in "the air"—the spiritual sphere between earth and heaven. Satan has worked in us all

and remains active in every unbeliever, tempting them with lies to doubt the existence of God's word, the truth of God's word and the motives behind God's word. He has been doing this ever since the Garden of Eden (Genesis 3:1-7). We were willingly persuaded by his lies because we were "disobedient" (Ephesians 2:2)—that is, we wanted the lies of the devil to be true so that we could continue being sinful. We'll learn more about satanic powers in chapter 6, because Christ's victory over them is a primary reason for Paul writing this letter and is therefore the reassuring climax to it.

3. "The cravings of our flesh" (v 3)—This word "flesh" does not mean just our physical body but our whole human nature. These cravings include our desperate appetites for exploitative pornography or selfish luxury as well as our incurably self-indulgent attention-seeking and proud self-glorification.

- **What was the result of this (v 1, 3b)?** "You were dead in your transgressions and sins" (v 1). Paul isn't just saying that we faced physical death, or even eternal spiritual "death" in separation from God in hell. He means that we were all born spiritually dead to God—utterly lifeless and insensitive to our Creator. Corpses can't do anything; they certainly cannot bring themselves to life.

  We were, therefore, "by nature deserving of wrath" (v 3—literally "children of wrath": God's punishment is our deserved inheritance). The wrath of God is not just an impersonal consequence, nor vindictive rage, but God's consistently pure anger towards evil, which means he will fairly punish sin. Paul is not describing any particularly degraded or decadent sector of our society, but all of us—for he says in verse 3: "All of us also lived among them". Although our genetic make-up, family upbringing and social circumstances determine precisely how we express our sinful nature, we all deserve to face God's wrath.

3. How do these verses show how desperate humanity's natural state is? None of us can say: "I am a good person". Without God we are spiritually dead, enslaved to worldly cultures, Satan's influence, and fleshly desires, and we should now be facing an eternity of suffering in hell. By nature, we are dead. If we don't really accept or appreciate this, we'll never really appreciate our salvation or praise our Saviour.

4. "But … God…" (v 4). Verse 3 is not the end of the story, because God has done something about our plight. What has he done (v 4-6)? God's mercy is revealed in three stages of resurrection, with cosmic implications:

1. He "made us alive" (v 5)—through faith in Jesus, we share in his representative death and resurrection as our King. Therefore, the resurrecting power of his Spirit breathes out his word in regenerative power. We're now like light bulbs plugged into the mains power of a light socket as Jesus electrifies us with his spiritual life.
2. He "raised us up" (v 6)—in our representative King we've already been accepted into heaven when Jesus was raised. If Wayne Rooney scores a winning penalty for England, only one man kicks the ball, but all of England win the game! Likewise, when our captain, Jesus, died and rose, we died and rose with him. Since heaven is now our present dwelling,

it must be our future destination.

3. He has "seated us with him in the heavenly realms" (v 6)—we're already seated with Jesus in his position of unique authority at the Father's right hand in the heavenly realms. Like places reserved at a wedding banquet in accordance with the groom's seating plan, seats are reserved for us by Jesus at his wedding feast. Since he has already sat down, it is as if we have sat down, because our places are secured by him!

- **Why (v 7)?** So that "in the coming ages he might show the incomparable riches of his grace". God wants to spend eternity showering us with blessings! God's great plan isn't just an exercise in tidying up the mess, or in putting down humanity's rebellion. His plan is to forever pour out a torrent of kindness upon us in heaven, and demonstrate for ever in the spiritual dimension the wisdom of his grace revealed in the cross. Every day, we shall be flooded with fresh blessings of his grace to explore and to prompt us to praise our Saviour.

5. Which words describe God's character (v 4-7)? What does each mean?
- Love (v 4): God's commitment to bless us for ever in Christ.
- Mercy (v 4): God withholding the punishment we deserve because Christ endured it for us on the cross.
- Grace (v 5, 7, 8): God generously giving us what we need in the obedience of Christ even unto death.
- Kindness (v 7): God's compassion in shrinking himself down to become one of us to exchange places with us on the cross!

Note: It may well be a good idea at this point to stop the study and spend time praising God for his love, mercy, grace and kindness.

6. How are people not saved? How are people saved (v 8-9)? It is "not by works … no one can boast" (v 9). We're not saved as a reward for our good deeds, our religious performance, or our church ministry. We were not saved, and will never be kept saved, by our good works of service, but by Christ's good works of service. It is by grace alone. Our salvation is entirely God's generous and costly gift. We receive it "through faith … the gift of God" (v 8). God's grace is the whole origin of our salvation—the faith created in us by his work is what enables us to receive his salvation.

- **So what is the wrong response to being saved (v 9)?** We've nothing to boast about, ie: place our confidence in (except the cross of Christ, Galatians 6:14)—whether in cocky self-confidence before God, arrogance towards unbelievers, or competition with other Christians. **And the right one (v 10)?** We are now "created in Christ Jesus to do good works". We've been recreated by God's Spirit through for a purpose—to do the good works prepared for us to do, in gratitude to God. To know that I've been saved for good works prepared by God liberates me from a lazy and loveless disengagement from the needs of the world, especially for the gospel, and also from ever feeling insignificant or useless.

EXPLORE MORE
Read Ezekiel 37 v 1-14. How is Ezekiel's vision a dramatic visual illustration of what Paul is talking about in Ephesians 2 v 1-10? This valley of death represented the spiritual condition of Israel—living people who were, spiritually speaking, just bones: utterly dead. And we all live in that valley, in villages, towns and cities full of apparently healthy people who are really spiritual skeletons, utterly dead to God.

Yet in Ezekiel's vision, the skeletons were brought to life by God's word and Spirit, becoming a vast army serving the Lord, just as Christians around the world have been regenerated by God's Spirit through God's gospel, brought to life in the living Christ. **How does it reinforce both the desperate situation of humanity, and the amazing power of God?** Again, we need to appreciate that dead bones cannot become living people by their own will, strength or power. We do not tend to see the world in this way, nor that this is what we were, and would still be without God's intervention. Equally, this image enables us to further grasp just how amazing God's intervention is. To turn a valley of skeletons into living, breathing people is a mere picture of the spiritual reality of what he has done for his people—for us—in Christ.

7. APPLY: Think about what would happen to your view of God and of yourself if you lost sight of:
- v 1-3?   • v 4-10?

This question is intended to reinforce the truth that to truly understand and enjoy (and live out) the gospel, we must understand how utterly helpless we were, and how totally raised we are. We must remember both that we were lifeless, and that now we have eternal life. You could ask your group which they find harder to remember (it may vary depending on whether they are at home or at work or at church; what life is throwing at them; and so on).

8. How does verse 12 describe the Gentiles' desperate state?
Note: these verses are fairly complex, and you won't have time in this study to fully

unpack them. There is more detail given in Ephesians For You, pages ??-??. But in summary, the Gentiles (ie: everyone who wasn't part of Old Testament Israel) were:

- "Separate from Christ" (v 12): Gentiles had no share in the benefits of the exciting promises to the Jewish people of a great Christ (or "Messiah", meaning "anointed" or "chosen" one), the divine peace-making King who, after centuries of Israel waiting for him, had now arrived in Jesus.
- "Excluded from citizenship in Israel" (v 12): Gentiles had no right to citizenship among the people of God. We had no rights to the privileges of Israel in knowing God or his covenant promises, his ethical laws, his powerful protection or his faithful provision.
- "Foreigners to the covenants of the promise" (v 12): God made one marvellous gospel promise to Abraham, that he and his descendants would enjoy the blessings of God's kingdom (Genesis 12 v 1-3), which was amplified periodically by covenant arrangements revealed progressively throughout the history of God's people.
- "Without hope and without God in the world" (v 12): In the face of death, there was only despair and no hope, because there was no relationship with God.

9. "But now…" (v 13). What has changed, and how has it changed (v 13-18)? We who once were far from God and his people have been "brought near" to God and his people—through Jesus' self-sacrifice for our sins. Christ has united the two most deeply separated categories of humanity in world history, Jews and Gentiles, into one entirely new people, central to his Father's grand plan to unite all things under him (v 14, 16).

The "barrier" or "dividing wall of hostility"

(v 14) between Jew and Gentile was the Law of Moses, which the Jewish religious leaders had turned from being a sign to the world of the goodness of God into a barrier excluding the world from God's good government. It was dismantled by Christ, who fulfilled all the terms of the law in his life, and then in his death exhausted its condemnation of both Jew and Gentile. And so Jesus can now preach "peace", both with God and with each other, to "you who were far away and … to those who were near" (v 17)—ie: to the Gentiles and to the Jews. We all share access to our Father on the same basis—"through him" (v 18), by the work of the same Spirit.

10. Where does God now dwell (v 21-22)? In his people—the church. By his Spirit, God lives in the people he has brought into his "holy temple", his church.

- **What is this new "temple" constructed upon (v 20)?** The foundation is "the apostles and prophets". The heavenly church, expressed in all its local congregations on earth, is founded upon the teaching of the first-century apostles of Christ, who announced the gospel of God, and the first-century prophets, who explained the word of God (see 4 v 11). So the foundation is finished (it should never be changed); and it is sufficient (we never need add to it). And the cornerstone of the whole building is Christ.

11. APPLY: How can there be lasting peace between enemies? Only in the "new humanity" that Christ has begun through his life, death and resurrection; only as we come to God through him, as forgiven sinners. Lasting peace is only possible when people realise their own desperate state, no matter their cultural background or moral performance, and by God's grace are given faith in the risen Jesus for forgiveness and eternal life. Lasting peace is only possible as we learn to see ourselves as Christ's people first and foremost; still British, or Palestinian, or Israeli, or whatever—still as white, black and so on—but supremely as followers of the Lord Jesus.

How is this expressed in your own church? Depending on your church and your cultural context, you may like to focus on how/whether your church displays (or could display) unity in Christ across cultural, ethnic, national or socio-economic "divides"; and/or on how you express unity

on a personal level by serving humbly and forgiving Christianly.

12. APPLY: How would you now define "grace" (try to include the truths of v 11-22 in your answer, as well as v 1-10)? What difference will it make in your lives as individuals and as a church? This refers back to Q1. Answers may be different among your group, and that is fine. Do encourage each member to think of specific ways in which a greater appreciation of God's grace to them as a church and as individuals will change their attitudes and/or actions in the coming week.

---

4 Ephesians 3
MYSTERY REVEALED

THE BIG IDEA

Every church is a trophy cabinet, displaying to the spiritual realms God's grace and wisdom in saving Jews and Gentiles in Christ. We have God's Spirit working in us to make us fit homes for Christ, and enable us to grasp more fully the love of Christ.

SUMMARY

The apostle Paul explains in 3 v 1-13 that there had been a perplexing mystery troubling Israel for centuries, concerning God's salvation plan—a mystery now solved in the most astonishing and unexpected fashion by the coming of Christ. The solution to this mystery is displayed by local churches to the spiritual realms for all to admire God's wisdom.

Verses 2-13 are a tangent, as Paul breaks off from outlining how he prays for the

Ephesians in light of the great truths of chapter 2 (3 v 1) to explain what he means in saying he is a prisoner for their sake. So v 2-13 explain his ministry, the gospel he preaches, and how the "mystery" of salvation is now proclaimed to the heavenly realms, through local churches made up of diverse saved sinners displaying God's amazing wisdom; and how therefore the Ephesians should not be discouraged that Paul is in prison, because the message is out: the gospel is being proclaimed through the apostles' ministry, and is showcased through the trophy cabinet of grace that every church is.

In verse 14, Paul returns to telling the Ephesians how he prays for them. His prayer is for power. We're often anxious about asking for power—perhaps for fear of becoming like the "prosperity" preachers on

"The God Channel" who exploit the naïve by offering power to get rich or get healed to whoever has enough misguided faith to send them money. That is not the "power" Paul is praying for, but a different kind of power… "power through his Spirit in your inner being, so that Christ may dwell in your hearts" (v 16-17); "power … to grasp" or comprehend (v 18); and "his power that is at work within us" (v 20).

In essence, Paul is praying that his believing friends' hearts would become more and more fit dwelling places for our holy King, Jesus; and then that they would be able to know (not just intellectually but in how they feel and look at life) the unknowable love of God shown to them in the gospel of Christ. So this study is in two parts—both of which are extremely exciting! Your group will see what a privilege it is to be part of a local church that showcases God's grace, displaying his wisdom to the spiritual realms. And they will be excited to know what God's power is achieving in them, and to pray that that power would be at work in others in their church.

OPTIONAL EXTRA

Get a shoebox, cut a hole in the side, and place three chess pieces—a king, a queen and a bishop—inside. Group members have to reach their hand in, feel for twenty seconds, and then pass the box on without saying anything. Then ask:

- What type of items were in the box (chess pieces)
- What specific type of chess pieces were in there? (A harder question, not everyone may know)
- What colour chess pieces were in there? (Impossible to know)

Then open up the top of the box to confirm what was already guessed at, and reveal

what had been a total mystery (the colour of the pieces). In the Old Testament, the gospel had been this kind of mystery. Some parts were clear (eg: God's promises in Genesis 3 v 15 and 12 v 1-3); some parts could be guessed at; but *how* God would bless the nations by reversing the effects of human sin was a mystery.

GUIDANCE FOR QUESTIONS

1. What is your favourite mystery (either novel, film, or "legend")? Be prepared to give your own favourite(s) first.

- **Why do you think we love mysteries, and why do we like discovering the solution?**

2. What exactly was the mystery made known to Paul (v 3-6)?
V 4: The "mystery of Christ"—a secret plan that was solved by and revealed in the death of Christ.
V 6: It is that through the gospel, Gentiles and Jews can be saved, without keeping the law of Israel, through faith in Christ, who kept the law for us and died for our lawbreaking. So now both Jews and Gentiles are:

- heirs together (the original text doesn't mention "with Israel"). We stand to inherit God's eternal kingdom, as part of his new people.
- members of one body: we are all united as part of God's church, and we are all equally part of that body. No one is more or less useful or special to it.
- sharers "in the promise in Christ Jesus": Paul is referring to the empowering of the Spirit, whose presence was promised in the OT as the chief blessing of being the people of God (Ezekiel 36 v 26-27), and who now lives in anyone who believes the gospel (Ephesians 1 v 13-14).

- **How did Paul know the solution to the mystery (v 3, 5)?** It was revealed to Paul "by revelation" (v 3). He had not worked it out or invented it; God had revealed it to him, through his Spirit (v 5). Note that Paul's gospel was not new—the gospel of blessing for all nations in God's kingdom had been announced to Abraham, and promised by the prophets. What was "new" was how God had brought that blessing. Paul's gospel was not a new gospel, but the ancient gospel revealed.

EXPLORE MORE

We are "heirs together"—but what are we heirs to? Read Revelation 22 v 1-5. What is wonderful about our inheritance? There is much to enjoy and be excited about here! Some aspects to notice:

- "The river of the water of life" depicts an inexhaustible torrent of life-giving spiritual abundance, forever washing us clean and filling us with thirst-quenching satisfaction from the Holy Spirit (see Ezekiel 47 v 1-12; John 7 v 38).
- "The tree of life" (literally the "wood" of life) symbolises the everlasting deliverance of the cross, and the leaves of this tree "are for the healing of the nations" (Revelation 22 v 2), permanently healing us from the damage of sin in our souls and the decay of death in our bodies. As the tree of life in the Garden of Eden was the source of life that looked forward to the cross on which Jesus was punished for our sins, the tree of life in the new creation looks back to the cross as the source of eternal life.
- "His servants [including us] will serve him", see him and rule with him. What a joy to finally serve him well. Just imagine seeing the face of your Saviour!

How would meditating on being heirs of all this have encouraged Paul

in prison (Ephesians 3 v 1), and the Ephesian church in a pagan city? Our view of our future always affects our feelings in our present, and often influences our actions too (just think about how you feel when you are at work shortly before going away on holiday). Whether we are in prison or a minority in a sea of pluralism and paganism, knowing how wonderful our inheritance is will change every Christian's perspective.

3. What is Paul's role in the revealing of this mystery (v 7-9)? He is a servant (literally slave) of the gospel (v 7), with the particular role of telling the Gentiles "the boundless riches of Christ" (v 8; see Acts 9 v 15) as he explains to everyone the "administration" (or "strategy") of this mystery—that is, as he explains to people how, through the life, death and resurrection of Jesus Christ, God is able to forgive and give eternal glory to both Jew and Gentile alike.

4. What amazing truth do we discover about our churches in verses 10-11? This is simply breathtaking. The local church displays to the heavenly realms "the manifold wisdom of God". The triumph of God's eternal plan to gather a diverse people into his kingdom under Christ is seen in every local church. Every local church gathering anywhere in the world is like one of those open-top bus champions' celebrations: but instead of a football team celebrating a temporary sporting victory in a stadium, a church gathering under Christ is a celebration of God's eternal spiritual victory over Satan, sin and death at the cross.

5. So how does Paul, who is in prison (v 1), see his sufferings (v 13)? He views them as being "for you"—in other words, necessary for his mission to preach the gospel to the Gentiles, and then build up Gentile believers (such as the Ephesians) in their faith. And it is all part of the way in which God is bringing things together under Christ (v 10). Paul is not downhearted about his imprisonment.

- **How should the Ephesians see his sufferings (v 13)?** Likewise, the Ephesians should "not … be discouraged". The news is out—the gospel has been heard, and the church in Ephesus is a trophy cabinet of God's grace to sinners.

6. APPLY: How does this passage change:

- **how we feel about meeting as church?** We may meet in a crumby school hall, a medieval stone building, or a leaky corrugated-iron hut. We may be growing in number, or very few. We may go unnoticed by those who live around us who get on with their lives as though our church isn't there. BUT we do not go unnoticed in the heavenly realms. There we are viewed as an advertisement of the triumph of God's plan to save sinners; his wisdom and power are on display. We need to realise that when we gather as church, there is nothing more important or more amazing going on anywhere in the world (apart from in other churches!).

- **how we view the prospect of suffering in order to share the gospel message?** The reality (or even the prospect) of suffering often stops us from being willing to share the gospel with colleagues, friends or family. We need to recognise that suffering hostility is part of gospel proclamation; to remember that persecution is not a sign of failure in our witness; and to keep explaining how the mystery of salvation has been solved at

the cross, and how the boundless riches of Christ are on offer, whether or not that puts us in prison. We need to care more about whether or not the gospel is being proclaimed than whether or not we are living comfortably.

7. What does Paul ask the Father to give the Ephesian Christians (v 16, 18, 20—notice the repeated word)? Power.

8. What does he ask God to do through the power of his Spirit? Try to put Paul's requests into your own words.

- **v 16-17:** To enable these believers to welcome Christ, and then to change so that Christ would be able to make himself at home in their hearts. By his Spirit, Christ lives in us from the moment we believe the gospel (1 v 13-14). But the word "dwell" doesn't just mean to arrive, but to settle down. Paul is praying that Christ would make himself the centre of their affections, decisions and behaviour—that they would change deeply to become a fit dwelling place for their perfect King.

- **v 18-19:** To appreciate the vast scale and immensity of Christ's love for them. This is something that can only happen by God's power, not our own effort, since it involves knowing something that surpasses knowledge. Paul prays that as we experience more and more of Jesus' love for us—as we look back at the cross where he died for us, and experience his love for us in helping us in the present— we would know the unknowable, and live with the confidence of being people who are so greatly, infinitely loved.

9. Why can we realistically hope to become suitable dwellings for the perfect Christ; and to truly know the

unknowable love of Christ (v 20-21)?
Because God is able to do all we can think of, and more. In our own strength and by our own initiative, we would never be able to transform ourselves, nor even begin to grasp the magnitude of the love God has for us in Christ. But it is not about our ability; it is about God's and he is more powerful than we can begin to appreciate. He can do what we cannot.

10. APPLY: How do these verses help us when:
- **we don't know what to pray for?**
- **we begin to think prayer doesn't work?**
- **we feel inadequate as believers?**
- **we feel we are unloved or misunderstood?**

Depending on your group and how much time you have, you might like to pick just one or two of these to focus on. Make sure your group identify specific verses in the passage to answer them.

11. APPLY: Remember where Paul is as he prays this joyful, hope-filled, ambitious prayer. How does that both encourage and challenge us as we consider our own lives, and prayer lives? Paul is in prison! Life is never too hard to be able to pray, or to pray boldly; God is never unable to come through for us. And life is never too hard to pray for others, rather than only for ourselves and our circumstances. We need to challenge ourselves and each other to pray unselfish, ambitious prayers, not based on our own situation, but on the character and power of the One to whom we're speaking.

5 Ephesians 4 v 1-16
HOW CHURCHES GROW

THE BIG IDEA
Churches grow as God wants them to—spiritually—as they work at maintaining their unity, as every member contributes their Christ-given gifts to the ministry, and as they encourage one another to grow in maturity.

SUMMARY
In Ephesians 4 v 1-16, Paul explicitly outlines the fundamental principles of how God grows churches in all times and all places. Remember that Paul's letter to the Ephesians is a "game of two halves". Chapters 1 – 3 have celebrated God's eternal plan: to gather all things in heaven and on earth together under Christ (chapter 1); through

the death and resurrection of Christ, which reconciles us to God and to each other (chapter 2); to manifest his triumphant wisdom to the spiritual realms in his church (chapter 3). Now, in chapters 4 – 6, Paul is explaining how his readers must live as a church committed to gathering people under Christ. He outlines three basic ingredients for church growth here in 4 v 1-16.

These fundamental principles of genuine spiritual growth are the same for every church in every context. There's nothing weird or complicated here. The prayerful and careful application of these principles will take time and sacrifice, but this is how

God always grows his churches. The three themes clarified here are: *unity* in *ministry* for *maturity*. We are all (not just our leaders) to work hard to remain united; to humbly contribute our gifts in ministry; and to speak the truth in love to help each other grow into Christ-like maturity. This is how God gathers people into churches under Christ!

OPTIONAL EXTRA

Gather together a few Lego models of a similar size and complexity, and have a "Lego race" by splitting your group into teams and then seeing who can build their model quickest. Give one person/pair only pieces that are all the same, or only two or three types. Draw out the fact that you can't build a workable, useful Lego model with only two or three types of brick. And then point out we often view church like this—that only certain "types" are really useful or have much to contribute. But churches are deliberately made up of different people with different gifts—and they become all God wants them to be as they all play their part, as we'll see in this passage. You could simply play the "race" at this point, and come back to the point after Q8 or 12.

GUIDANCE FOR QUESTIONS

1. How do people think churches grow? What do you think? This is, deliberately, a question that can be answered in different ways! We might think of growth as numerical. Many churches seek to follow the priorities, preaching styles or programmes of other churches whose size has rapidly increased. Or we might think of growth as in depth—greater maturity.

- **What might people mean by the phrase "a growing church"?** This question will help you recognise that there are different definitions of "growing".

2. Think back to the content of chapters 1 – 3. What is "the calling you have received"? It is a calling to:
- praise God as we enjoy our spiritual blessings in Christ (1 v 3)
- live as God's forgiven children, pure and blameless (1 v 4-5, 7)
- live under Christ's rule, as one day everything will (1 v 10)
- know God better, understand our hope more, and experience his power at work in us (1 v 17-20)
- do the good works God prepared for us to do as his new-creation people (2 v 10)
- proclaim God's wisdom to the heavenly realms (3 v 10).

- **What does verse 1 suggest Paul will be teaching us about in the rest of the letter?** "How to live a life worthy" of this identity that we now have. We will see what it means to live as part of God's family, under Christ's rule, in response to his grace, by the power of his Spirit in real life.

3. What do church members need to put effort into (v 3)? Protecting the "unity of the Spirit", which is the special togetherness that the Holy Spirit creates in a congregation through our "bond of peace". This is our shared experience of adoption into God's family for peace with God and peace with each other in Christ. We are to do everything we possibly can, in whatever roles we have, to pursue and maintain the unity of our church in Christ instead of fuelling division.

- **What three attitudes does Paul lay out in verse 2 which we need to adopt? Why does each require "effort"?**
  1. Being "humble". This is not the same as being quiet or shy or always speaking critically of ourselves. It means

restraining our sense of entitlement to be the focus of other people's care and attention by submitting ourselves to others with respect, in order to promote their best interests, eg: allowing someone else's teaching or musical talents to be more celebrated in our church than our own, or realising that our desire for attention from a leader may need to remain neglected while they are pressured with caring for others (who may be facing desperate crises we know little about).

2. Being "gentle" (literally "meek"). This is not being weak. It means dealing with other people with kindness rather than roughness, with empathetic compassion rather than demanding force, and with soft encouragement rather than hard bullying—for instance, urging people to raise their standards for Jesus' sake by setting a good example rather than cajoling people for our own agenda by criticism.

3. Being "patient" means to be long-suffering of the faults of others and slow in seeking to rebuke them, recognising that spiritual growth takes time and that we are all works in progress. We are called to be patient, for instance, when those who are younger in faith seem unreliable, lazy or demanding; or when we experience less love than we have tried to show to others.

4. How do verses 4-6 underline the special Spirit-given unity we have within our church? The repeated word here is "one". As Christians, we have so much in common—what unites us as God's people is far greater and more significant than the ways in which we are different.

5. APPLY: What are the biggest obstacles to this kind of gospel unity in your church? There are no right or wrong answers to this, and they will vary from church to church. Examples might include: the busy-ness of life; an exaltation of one "type" of person/ability/career choice/music style over another; sheer selfishness; competition between ministries within the church, etc.

• **How can you, as church members, be fostering unity?** Encourage your group to think not so much about what "the church" could do or "the leaders" should do, but about what they can do as individual members of the church.

6. What has each church member been given (v 7)? By whom? "Grace"—given by Christ.

• **Given that in verse 11-12 Paul goes on to talk about roles and abilities, what does "grace" mean in verse 7?** This "grace" here is not referring to God saving us by grace alone in Christ dying for us, but to his subsequent additional grace in giving us gifts of ministry as Christ has distributed them. These are given not for our personal satisfaction or reputation, but to enrich the life and service of others in our church. These gifts of grace are not just abilities but ministries—ways for us to serve his church family.

7. What is [the] job [of evangelists, pastors and teachers] (v 12)? To equip the people in their church for "works of service" (this word can also be translated "ministry" or "worship"). Teachers of every kind in the church have been given to the church by Jesus to equip all of us for our many different ministries, which will grow and build up the church, to glorify God.

What is the outcome of them doing this (v 12b-13)? The body of Christ—the church—is "built up". It is the works of "service" ("ministry") of God's people in the congregation that builds up the church in unity and maturity. It is as the whole church contributes its ministry that the church will: grow in "unity in the faith" (v 13)—a shared and true understanding of God revealed in Christ as he is revealed in the Bible; become "mature"—not be childish in our faith and in the way we live that out in our lives; and attain "to the whole measure of the fullness of Christ"—so we grow not only in doctrinal unity, but in becoming more and more like Jesus himself.

8. How does this undermine the idea that the full-time, paid pastors are there to do "ministry" for the rest of the church to "receive"? All of us have ministries and we are all ministers, because we are all being equipped by our Bible-teachers for our particular church-growth ministries! The pastors are there to encourage, challenge and equip us to identify how we can minister to our church, and to get going with that ministry. They are not there to do all the ministry.

9. APPLY: Why is it so easy to have a "consumer" mindset [rather than a "contributing" one]? First, because that is the way Western society works—church is seen as an entertainment option among many, or as a transaction, such as visiting the bank. Church becomes something that I go to in order to get blessed, as though I am a shopper filling my basket in the supermarket. Second, because we are naturally selfish—we ask: "What do I get from this?" rather than: "What can I give to this?" Third, because if a church's culture is consumerist, then young Christians in that

church will understandably come to think of church in that way. **In what ways do you see this in your attitude to your church?** Again, answers will vary from person to person. But encourage your group members to talk about themselves (not others), and to think of ways in which they can defeat consumerist attitudes once they have spotted them.

• **In what ways are you currently contributing your ministry to your church? How do these verses encourage you in these areas of ministry?** Sometimes we're better at seeing what we do badly than celebrating what we do well and praising God for his work in us. It is not wrong to identify areas where your members are serving humbly and sacrificially!

10. What will a church where every member is contributing to the ministry:
• **not do (v 14)?** They will not be susceptible to false teaching and following fashionable but passing fads.

• **do (v 15)?** They will speak the truth in love, and as they do so, they will grow in maturity—ie: to be like Christ. We are all to speak truthfully and lovingly. We are to counsel each other appropriately in how the gospel affects our lifestyle, decisions and attitudes. We are to challenge each other when we fear that a fellow believer is not living according to the truth in some way. Biblical conversations are a form of Bible-teaching that helps people to mature in Christ-likeness.

However, this is not an excuse for us to say all the hard and horrible things we want to say to someone we dislike or find frustrating, or to pull ourselves up by pulling others down, or to sit in judgment and exercise control over other people with our advice. Instead, we should want to bring people to the word of Christ for his counselling, recognising that none of us are perfect and that we are all continually in need of biblical counselling.

11. How does the image of the church that Paul gives in verse 16 underline all that he's been saying in this passage? Each local church is a body, growing as it's held together by its ligaments and as "each part does its work". And it all comes "from him", its head, the Lord Jesus Christ (v 15). This image of the body underlines: the unity of the congregation, and the importance of maintaining that unity; the need for every single church member to serve the whole in whatever way they can, which will be different to other members; and that Bible-teachers in the church are like "ligaments", supporting the body and enabling it to grow, but not the only active parts of the body.

EXPLORE MORE
Read 1 Corinthians 12 v 12-31. What ideas that you've seen in Ephesians 4 does Paul develop in this passage? The church is one body, with many different parts. All the parts need one another, because they are varied and interdependent. We all need all of us to be serving our body. The church has been brought together by God, in a deliberate way.
Why does thinking of church as one body with many parts help you not to think too highly of yourself as a church member, or too little? I will not think too highly of myself because I know that I am just one member of a greater part, the body, given my gifts not to look good but to serve, and that I need all the other parts of the body to be at work if I am to flourish. I will not think too little of myself because I

know that God has put together my church in such a way that it needs me; my church's growth depends in part on me contributing my unique gifts to the body.
How far is verse 26 a description of your church, and your own attitude to others in your church?

12. APPLY: What part are you or could you be playing as individuals and a group, in:
• **keeping and nurturing unity?**
• **contributing your ministry?**
• **growing in maturity as you speak truth in love?**
Again, do identify and praise God for the ways in which your church and your group members within your church are already doing these three things. Then move on to thinking in specific, practical ways how you can each (or as a group) promote unity, contribute ministry, and speak truth in love.

6 Ephesians 4 v 17 – 5 v 20
CHRISTIANS ARE NOT CHAMELEONS

THE BIG IDEA

We must live out our calling to be God's children. This means not living as the world does or as we used to, but imitating God and living in love—our conduct with sex and alcohol are two areas in which we do this.

SUMMARY

Christians often live like spiritual chameleons, imitating the world around us in order to remain camouflaged and safe from spiritual predators who might criticise or hurt us. We can usually tell that we're spiritual chameleons when unbelievers who have spent time with us are shocked to discover that we're Christians. So Paul challenges all of us: "You must no longer live as the Gentiles do…" (v 17). In this passage, he is saying: *Stop copying the world like chameleons and start imitating God* (5 v 1).

Verse 17 begins "So"—meaning in the light of what Paul has said in chapters 1 – 3; and also in the light of what he's said so far in chapter 4, calling us to "a life worthy of the calling you have received" (v 1), by preserving our unity and contributing our ministry to grow in maturity. But most immediately, "so" follows v 16, where Paul says Christ's church body grows "as each part does its work". The obvious response is: "Paul, can you be more specific about this work? What do you want us to do?"

In these verses, Paul lays out how we do our work. It involves:

• *Not living as those around us do (v 17-19):* Paul paints a bleak picture of the non-Christian life as futile in thinking, darkened in understanding, hard of heart, separated from real life lived in relationship with God, and continually seeking satisfaction through sin, but never finding it.

• *Taking off our old self and putting on our new self (4 v 20 - 5 v 2):* by having become a man to show us what a righteous life looks like (as well as to live that life on our behalf), God's Son teaches us how to live worth of our calling. We need to become more holy—more like him—through taking off our old grubby character, being renewed in our thinking by his Spirit, and becoming more Christ-like in our character. Verses 29-32 give a list of ways in which we do this.

• *Avoiding all sexual immorality and giving thanks for the gift of sex (5 v 3-7):* this includes in how we speak as well as in what we do, and Paul warns us that ongoing, unrepentant sexual immorality leaves us outside God's kingdom.

• *Living in the light, not the darkness (5 v 8-20):* so that we can expose the darkness by showing those around us a distinctive, better way to live. We are not to be filled/influenced by alcohol, for instance, but by the Spirit, giving thanks to God and singing and speaking his praises to those around us.

Note: In this study, you will be discussing the area of sexual morality. Bear in mind that this may be a delicate subject for some members of your group, either because of issues they are currently facing, or because of circumstances they have been through in their past. Be sensitive as you go through the study, and make sure you follow up with anyone who needs caring for.

OPTIONAL EXTRA

The passage includes the image of taking off our old selves/clothes, and putting on new selves/clothes. Our clothes show something of who we are; and they affect how we behave. So show the group some pictures of people from around the world in their national dress, and challenge them to guess which country they are each from. Discuss how wearing the national dress might make someone feel, and/or behave differently. Alternatively, for a more light-hearted start, ask group members to bring in photos of themselves as teenagers, wearing clothes that were fashionable then, but may well no longer be!

GUIDANCE FOR QUESTIONS

1. How might Christians live like spiritual chameleons? The possible answers to this question are virtually endless! But here are some possibilities:

- We may be consciously copying someone else: a popular friend, a successful colleague, an exciting celebrity or impressive public figure.
- We may have a spiritually damaging fixation with salary and status,
- We may have a spiritually unhealthy tendency to uncritically approve of ungodly religious opinions, because of a fear of appearing "judgmental".
- If we're unhappily single or unhappily married, we may surrender to bitter self-pity and indulge our appetites for erotic fantasy, because we've accepted the lies of our media that we're all entitled to sexual pleasure, stunted without it, and free to seek it in private without censure.
- **Why might Christians live like spiritual**

chameleons? To remain safe from criticism or rejection. It's much easier and popular to blend in with our surroundings, particularly if and when we are the only Christian in the workplace, at the sports club or in the pub, or in a conversation with others, etc.

- **How can we tell if we are living like spiritual chameleons?** We can usually tell if we're spiritual chameleons when unbelievers who have spent time with us are shocked to discover that we're Christians.

2. What does Paul means by living "as the Gentiles do" (v 17-19)? He means:

- to think like non-Christians—"in the futility of their thinking" (v 17). This might mean empty worship or superstitious idolatry; or accepting the empty platitudes of popular folk religion (eg: that a deceased atheist relative is "happily smiling down on us" or "lives forever in our hearts"). Or it may be the empty confidence that whichever God exists, he'll look at my good points and let me into heaven.
- to "be darkened in their understanding … separated from the life of God because of… the hardening of their hearts" (v 18): Futile thinking is caused by spiritual blindness. It's a spiritual matter of the heart, not an intellectual issue. So naturally, no one has relational knowledge of God (**Note:** Paul explains more about why and how our hearts are hardened in Romans 1 v 18-21).
- this futile thinking caused by hardened hearts results in a life without sensitivity (the relationship to God we were created for), directed by sensuality (shameless debauchery), indulging in impurity (riotous immorality), and being full of greed (insatiable appetites, because sin never

truly satisfies).

Notice that Paul is saying that a Christian, although the Spirit has given them new hearts and a relationship with God, can still think in this futile way, and is still influenced by these appetites.

3. What difference does becoming a Christian make (v 20-24)?

- We have been taught (by Jesus in the way he lived his life) to take off our "old self, which is being corrupted by its deceitful desires" (v 22). We must learn consciously to put aside the lifestyle we previously lived in.
- Getting undressed in this way prepares us to be "made new in the attitude of [our] minds" (v 23). As we reject corrupted opinions, the Spirit of God will renew our attitudes within us through his word, so that new affections are created within us. We can't just aim to get rid of all desires—rather, our filthy desires must be replaced with clean desires. This is a process that begins at conversion, but continues throughout our lives.
- We have learned, and must keep practising, the putting on of our "new self" (v 24). This means becoming more and more like Jesus—it is "to be like God". Jesus is righteous in his generous love and holy in his disciplined purity—we need to "put on" this kind of attitude and behaviour.

So being a Christian makes a complete difference not only to our eternity, but to our outlook and conduct right now. It is as different as changing our whole wardrobe. We must expect to be dressed utterly differently to how we were before God saved us, and to how those around us who don't know God are "dressed".

4. What distinctions between "old self"

living and "new self" living does Paul highlight in verses 25-32?

- *Falsehood vs speaking truthfully* (v 25): because "we are all members of one body". We must be honest with each other, like people belonging to one body of Christ. This requires speaking truthfully about each other (no more gossiping or damning with faint praise), speaking truthfully to each other (no more exaggeration and lying), and being conscious of the truth of the gospel of grace (no more hypocritical criticism).
- *Sinful anger vs (implicitly) forgiveness* (v 26-27): Paul recognises that it is sometimes appropriate to be angry—for instance, when our brothers and sisters in Christ around the world are being persecuted, or if someone has been hurt by someone else in our church. But we're not to indulge our anger so that it becomes self-important righteous indignation. Paul says it's wise to adopt a time limit for grievances—to give up our causes and campaigns by the end of any day, so that Satan can't gain an opportunity to build up divisive factions that destroy the church over time.
- *Stealing, and a "taking" attitude vs working hard in order to live out a "giving" attitude* (v 28): Paul recognises that in the godless lifestyle we once lived in, we may have been stealing: whether permanently "borrowing" tools from work that we never return, or over-charging clients, or falsely claiming expenses or avoiding taxes. Christians have to stop sharp practices and work hard, not to spend excessively on ourselves, but to contribute to the needs of others in our family and church, and beyond that to gospel work, especially among the poor. We are no longer to use our hands to get, but to give.
- *Unwholesome talk vs building-up talk*

(v 29): The word "unwholesome" is literally "rotten"—it refers to vulgar jokes, damaging gossip or spiteful criticism, which needs to be replaced with wholesome language and words that encourage and strengthen the faith of others.

- *No more grieving the Holy Spirit (v 30):* Paul refers here to the rebellions of Israel, on their way to the promised land, which so grieved the Spirit of God (Isaiah 63 v 10). We who have been sealed with his Spirit as belonging to God are not to grieve him by repeatedly rebelling against God with endless discontented grumbling and moral disobedience.
- *No more bitterness, rage, slander, malice (v 31):* we can gradually replace all our malicious instincts towards those who annoy, hurt, mock or malign us with a little of the grace that Christ showed towards his enemies, including us.

5. Who is our great model in living like this (4 v 32 – 5 v 2)? God himself. We can learn to be generously kind, gently compassionate and mutually forgiving from the way that God has graciously forgiven us (v 32). Rather than being chameleons, we are to imitate God (5 v 1), especially in demonstrating the sacrificial love he has shown us, supremely in Christ's death (v 2).

6. APPLY: Why do we tend not to see "Gentiles" in the way Paul does? Some possible reasons (your group may come up with others, and not mention all of these):

- We see their moral goodness or that they are fun to be around, and we forget that what matters far more is their hardened rejection of God.
- We see our own faith as a feature of our life rather than the foundation of our life. So we don't see ourselves as very different

from others—it's just a lifestyle choice rather than the most important part of who we are.

- It is inconvenient—if we view Gentiles in the way Paul does, then we have no excuse for not seeking to speak to them about Jesus, which can be costly. It's far easier to convince ourselves that they are not really separated from the life of God.

- **How would thinking more like Paul affect our pursuit of holiness and our desire to evangelise?**
  - We would be far less quick to compromise—to live as spiritual chameleons. We would be better at identifying ways in which we are being influenced by the world rather than our Lord; and we would be more serious about repenting of times when we have lived "as the Gentiles do". In other words, recognising how differently God calls us to think, feel and live would mean we pursued holiness in a more wholehearted way.
  - We would also, of course, be more committed to evangelism if we truly believed that our non-Christian family members and friends were losing out now (because their lives would never be truly satisfied) and were facing eternity without God.

7. APPLY: Choose the two old-self/ new-self differences that you think are most challenging in your culture. What would it look like to be chameleons in each area? How can you encourage one another to live Christ-like lives in each area? You may wish to choose the two differences to discuss here that would be most relevant to your group. Alternatively, divide your group into pairs, ask them to consider one or two differences, and then "report back" to the group. Make sure you talk practically, and specifically, rather than in abstract ways.

8. What does it mean to "live a life of love" (v 2)? To give ourselves up. True love is about voluntary self-sacrifice, particularly when it is directed at others' salvation or blessing. Our love is to be Christ shaped, not culture shaped. And it is to be done to please God "as a fragrant [ie: pleasing] offering". Notice that our ethic is not just the absence of wickedness but the presence of love; not just the rejection of impurity but the practice of grace towards others. Bible-believing Christians often have a reputation for what we deny and reject, but not a matching reputation for gracious generosity towards others.

9. What does this mean God's holy people must not even indulge a hint of (v 3-4)?
- Sexual immorality: any sexual activity outside marriage. This includes watching porn, reading erotic novels, visiting strip shows, lusting, and so on.
- Impurity: a broader vice that includes lust but also licentious behaviour such as drunkenness, crudeness, etc.
- Greed: an unrestrained desire for material things—an attitude that makes us covetous of what others have, and bitterness about what we don't have.
- Obscenity, foolish talk or coarse joking: in other words, any conversation that makes light of immorality. It is not only that we must avoid these things in how we live, but we must avoid laughing about or legitimising them in what we say and what we smile about.

- **Is verse 4 telling us as Christians to**

avoid talking about sex? Why/why not? No! We are to talk about sex, but to do so with "thanksgiving". The healthy alternative to hedonism is "thanksgiving" (v 4). We can always be giving thanks to God for his overflowing generosity, especially in our extravagant spiritual blessings in Christ (1 v 1-14), whether or not we are having sex, or good sex, or enough sex. The fundamental solution to immorality, impurity and greed is nothing more complicated than thanksgiving, because sexual disobedience in Christians is generally caused to some degree by the spiritual amnesia of forgetting God's grace, and feeling sorry for ourselves and entitled to indulge our sinful appetites.

10. How does Paul underline the seriousness of these commands in verses 3-7?
- v 3: "These things are improper for God's holy people". If we want to be in God's family, we have to be different.
- v 5: Habitual, unrepentant behaviour of these sorts (note: Paul is not talking here about occasional, repented sins, but a settled lifestyle) means that, whatever we may think, we are outside God's kingdom
- v 6: Disobedience brings wrath. We mustn't think that we can disobey God in a repeated way that we never truly repent of or turn from, and not face his anger.
- v 6-7: It is very easy to be deceived on these things by people. Many—even within the church—like to ignore or "reinterpret" these words. But given Paul's warnings in v 3 and 5-6, we must not become "partners with" those who are disobedient.

EXPLORE MORE
Re-read Ephesians 5 v 8-14. What image

does Paul use here to describe the difference that becoming a Christian makes? Conversion is like stopping being "darkness", and becoming "light in the Lord" (v 8). And then the "light" grows "fruit" (v 9). In fact Paul uses three images here—we have come from darkness to light, so we are now children, and grow fruit!

What should a Christian do (v 10-11)? Find out what pleases the Lord (rather than living to indulge ourselves or pleasing others). **And not do?** We should have "nothing to do" with fruitless, non-Christian ways of living. (Paul is repeating his point from verse 3: not even "a hint.)

Why is it loving for a Christian not only to "have nothing to do" with sinful behaviour, but to "expose it" by living differently in an obvious way? Because then people around us see there is a different way to think and live. If we live in the "darkness", copying those around us, their assumptions will never be challenged. When we live differently, we begin to "expose" the false premises and empty promises of a "Gentile" way of living.

11. What else does Paul tell Christians not to do, and to do (v 18)? "Do not get drunk on wine." Although in moderation alcohol gladden the heart (Psalm 104 v 15), too much often leads to "debauchery". We are to enjoy God's gifts, but not to get drunk—whether this drunkenness takes place in a town centre, or at a respectable dinner party at a friend's home.

Then Paul says: *Do be filled with the Holy Spirit.* We are to be people who are "under the influence" of the Holy Spirit, not of alcohol—our affections and actions directed by him.

• **What are the signs that someone is "filled with the Spirit" (v 19—see also**

Colossians 3 v 16-17)? We joyfully sing to one another, to build each other up. And our hearts sing to the Lord. The Spirit works to make us emotional about the glory of the gospel.

The parallel passage in Colossians (3 v 16) explains that this happens as we let the Spirit's message of Christ, in the Scriptures, dwell richly in us.

12. APPLY: As a church, how can you more fully obey the words of v 3-4? Discuss how you can encourage each other; how you can hold each other accountable; how you can help one another in what you talk about; how you can speak positively about sex, rather than just not speaking about it at all.

• **How can you positively seek to love others as Christ did (v 2), rather than as the world does?** Again, there are many answers to this! Encourage your group to think about their own individual lives, and specific people/situations in which they can love sacrificially with the aim of saving or blessing others.

7 Ephesians 5 v 21 – 6 v 9
AT HOME AND AT WORK

THE BIG IDEA
Christians are able to, and called to, display Christ's triumph in saving and changing his people, and his love for his people, every day in their marriages, families and workplaces, through how they lead when they are called to, and how they submit when they are called to.

SUMMARY
Paul now turns to show how we can "live out "the calling [we] have received" (4 v 1)—the calling to enjoy and declare God's victory in Christ, in our homes and workplaces. And he is teaching Christians both to be loving, sacrificial leaders and to be loving, submitting followers, as they are called: husbands and wives (5 v 22-33), parents (particularly fathers) and children (6 v 1-4), employers and employees (6 v 5-9).

In each of these relationships, the person who is called to submit is addressed first, and then the person in authority—each time with an instruction followed by a motivation in Christ. Everyone will be accountable to him, and those he has redeemed will long to please him… and here we discover how we can do that.

Distinctively and radically for the time, the biblical principle of the equality and dignity of all persons is forcibly emphasised here. Each person is addressed as responsible before God for their own behaviour. In each relationship someone is required to exercise authority to lead, and the other is required to gladly submit to that leadership. None is more or less important than the other.

For those of us in Western 21st-century cultures, we need to realise that the Bible teaches that our role does not define our worth. Submitting to someone else does not mean we are worth less than them. This passage—perhaps particularly in its discussion on marriage—will challenge many of us, because of our culture's rejection both of Bible-defined marriage itself, and of our roles within it; and because we are sinful humans, who instinctively struggle to lead well (husbands) and submit gladly (wives), as our ancestors did in Eden (Genesis 3).

Note: This passage will look at some areas of life which may well be sensitive or deeply upsetting for members of your group, for different reasons: eg: they may be single, but desperately want to be married; or married, but deeply unhappy or regretful; or have adult children who have rejected their faith; or facing extremely difficult workplace situations. Do be aware of these issues as you work through the study, and do remind your group as you need to that our God is a God of grace, who forgives us when we sin and strengthens us to do good works in every situation. And do make space in your diary to follow up individually with anyone who might need further counsel and prayer.

OPTIONAL EXTRA
Since the focus of much of the study is on families… If all your group are married, then you could look at each others' wedding photos. Alternatively, ask everyone to bring in a photo of themselves as a baby, put them all on a table, and ask people to guess who is who.

GUIDANCE FOR QUESTIONS
1. What answers would you get if you

asked a hundred people:
- **What is the point of marriage?**
- **What is the most important aspect of parenting?**
- **Why do you go to work?**

If you want to and have time, you could ask what your group think 100 Christians would give as answers.

- **How would you (honestly!) answer each of those for yourself?** Do encourage honest answers, rather than the ones your group may feel they are "meant" to give!

2. Within marriage, what are wives instructed to do (v 22)? Submit. This means to arrange yourself under someone's authority and follow their leadership. This is not an enforced, servile oppression (as in some religious cultures and too often in the history of the church) but voluntary. Husbands are not called to *make* their wives submit.

- **What is her model (v 24)?** The submission of the church to Christ in everything. **How does this clarify what Paul means (and doesn't mean)?** The church submits to Christ gladly and voluntarily, even joyfully. We follow Christ's lead because we understand that his rule is for our best; we know that he loves us, sacrificially (which is what husbands are called to do—see Q3); we trust that he is guiding us wisely. So we respond with respect and thankfulness. But the church's submission to Christ does not mean that Christians lose their personalities, or never think for themselves or ask questions. And it does not mean that we always find it easy or natural to submit. So Paul is not calling wives to lay down their personalities, and never discuss or question anything. Neither is he

suggesting that submitting will always or often be easy. But it is "as to the Lord" (NIV84)—as part of her service of Christ, and in accordance with God's great plan to bring everything together under Christ (even though it is often sneered at today). This is a role, a temporary role in this world, required by her Lord.

3. We might expect husbands to be commanded to "lead" their wives. But what does Paul tell them to do (v 25)? To love their wives. Their leadership must flow from their love. Notice that the command to love is repeated three times (v 25, 28, 33). A husband is to be committed to loving his wife by serving her through leading her.

- **What is his model (v 25-27)?** Christ himself. And Jesus loved the church by giving himself up, even to death, for them (v 25). **How does this clarify what Paul means (and doesn't mean)?** A husband should take the initiative in sacrificially giving himself to the good of his wife. Loving like Christ means giving up his life even unto death; and until that is necessary, it means dying to what is easiest for him in countless little, everyday ways. A husband is to love his wife for better, for worse; for richer, for poorer; in sickness and in health—not just providing for her materially but giving himself to her, physically, emotionally and spiritually. And if his career, or even church ministry, is consistently making this impossible, then he should consider changing it for the sake of his wife.

The aim of a godly husband's love is his wife's best interests, which Paul explains from three aspects of Christ's love. First, Christ died to make his people "holy" (v 26)—devoted to God. Second, he died to "cleanse" us from sin, through the spiritual washing of the word of the gospel; and third, he died to present us to himself on the last day as "radiant" in the spiritual glory of Christ (v 27)—without any stain of sin or wrinkle of ungodliness or blemish of imperfection, but holy and blameless in spiritual beauty.

And this, says Paul, is to be a husband's chief goal for his wife. A husband is to be concerned, not primarily for his wife's short-term happiness (perhaps hoping for an easier life himself), but for her long-term holiness, cleansing and radiance in Christ.

4. What does Paul talk about in verse 31? Human marriage (Paul is quoting from the creation account in Genesis 2 v 24). **What does he then say he's talking about in verse 32?!** "Christ and the church." So Paul's deeper focus is not upon our marriages, but rather, the gospel—the "mystery" that people of every background are being united to Christ, who died for them, and reconciled to God.

• **How does this help us to avoid making too little, and too much, of a marriage between a man and a woman?** Western culture tends to think too little of marriage. It can be redefined according to society's opinions. Entering it is seen as a temporary decision rather than a life-long promise. If it does not make us happy, we are free to walk away. But as Christians, we understand that marriage is a God-given union, a life-long commitment, and, excitingly, part of the way in which the mystery of the gospel, the wonder of Christ's love for his people and his people's glad submission to him, is displayed to the heavenly realms and to the world. But equally, this passage reminds us not to

make too much of marriage or family. It is temporary (we are married till death us do part). And it is a picture of a much greater reality—the relationship between Christ and his church. If we have the happiest, most fulfilling of marriages, but are not part of Christ's church, then we are missing the greater reality. If we are not married, or are in (for whatever reason) a difficult marriage, then we need to remember that we can still enjoy, eternally, the greater relationship that marriage pictures. So we must not make marriage an idol, where it becomes too important and we compromise on our obedience to Christ and our commitment to our church because of it.

5. APPLY: How would your culture react to God's words on marriage here? This will depend on your cultural context. Western culture would react with horror to the idea of wives submitting (though don't assume your group won't think of ways in which the culture might react positively to parts of it). More traditional cultures may find it harder to see a husband's role as being one of loving, serving, sacrificial leadership. The gospel and its implications for our lives challenges both post-modern, modern and traditional cultures.

• **How do these verses help you to view and present God's view on marriage as positive, helpful and wise?** Here are some possibilities:
  • God's word here gives us a way to enjoy our marriages without putting too much pressure on them. It tells us that marriage is great, but not ultimate; that it can be wonderful, but will not be perfect.
  • God's word here is good news for those who are not married when they want

to be, or who are unhappily married, or who have been hurt by previous marriages—there is a relationship with Christ that surpasses by far the greatest experience of human marriage. So Christians who are not married are not "missing out".

- Submission fosters agreement rather than struggle. Instead of leaving marriages in confusion that too often becomes a battle between the strength of a man's bicep and the sharpness of a woman's tongue, God has provided for a consistently loving leadership and sensible submission in marriage that fits the way he has designed us differently as males and females.

6. APPLY: How can you, as a church, make sure you celebrate marriage for all that it is, without idolising it as something that it isn't? Discuss whether your church is tempted to make too little of marriage—perhaps by not clearly teaching what marriage is, who marriage is between, and what the wife's and husband's roles are; or by your conversations not encouraging one another to be loyal to your spouse, not joking about husbands being "under the thumb"; and in other ways. And discuss how your church might give the impression that marriage is "better"; how you might look unwelcoming or fail to make provision for those who are, for whatever reason, single mothers, unmarried, widows, divorced; and so on.

7. What are children who are still living at home to do (v 1)? "Obey your parents"—this command requires children to fully comply with their parents' instructions. This is obviously easier when those instructions are sensible and clearly explained, and when the children have

reason to trust that their parents love them. But children are naturally as sinful as their parents and so they not only need tons of disciplined love (not indulgence), but also loving discipline (not bullying).

⌄

- **What spiritual motivation does Paul give children?** They obey "in the Lord, for this is right" (v 1). Children don't have to obey parents because parents are more important than children (they aren't), but as part of a child's loving obedience to Christ. Within the limits of living for the Lord (not complying with immoral, idolatrous or anti-gospel requirements such as being forbidden to pray or follow Jesus), this command makes obeying parents not just the most peaceful thing to do, but the morally right thing to do. As a child clears the dishes or tidies their bedroom or comes home before midnight and struggles to understand why this is such a big deal for their parents, they need to remember that obeying their parents is the right thing because Jesus has asked them to do it, and that these are opportunities to please their Saviour.
- **If you're a parent, do you help your children to have this motivation for their obedience to you? How can you do this?**

- **What does it mean for adult children to obey verse 2, do you think?** The word "honour" means serious respect and is commonly translated "fear" or "reverence". For adults, this means respecting our parents' wisdom by seeking and heeding their advice; it will mean caring for them by visiting, providing practical care and financial help, and possibly accommodating them as they become more frail, unwell and afraid. Just as we will not allow our kids to disrespect our spouse, we must not disrespect our own parents or parents-in-law in the way we talk about them.

8. What are fathers (and mothers, in support of the father or in their place if the father is not present) to do, and not do (v 4)?

• Do "bring them up in the training and instruction of the Lord". The words "bring them up" mean to "nourish" or nurture children. This implies long term relational care and not rapid mechanistic results. The word "training" means corrective discipline. And "instruction of the Lord" means that godly dads will be trying to make time at home to read and discuss how to apply Biblical principles to daily life and for quality conversations to happen naturally. They will partner with their church's children and youth leaders—but not entirely delegate their responsibility of raising their children to know the gospel to them.
  Note: Paul is not saying that it is a father (and mother)'s job to *make* their children be Christians—as though it is the parents' fault if the child grows up to reject Christ. It *is* the father's responsibility to make sure their children grow up knowing and understanding the gospel, and what the Bible says about who Jesus is, and what it means to trust and obey him.

• Do not "exasperate your children". Fathers shouldn't provoke their children to anger with severe or relentless discipline, unreasonably harsh demands, inconsistent or unfair rules, constant criticism or humiliation, or insensitivity to different seasons of a child's weaknesses, fears and needs. The best antidote to exasperating our children, whether difficult toddlers or grumpy teenagers, is to consciously resolve to enjoy them as precious gifts from God for a short season—to recall that we were all kids once, and to remember how patient our heavenly Father has been with us when we were defiant and grumpy!

9. APPLY: How can parents prioritise bringing your children up "in the training and instruction of the Lord"? How can the church help in this?

Use this question as an opportunity to share ideas and struggles. Make sure the discussion is positive, and that the more confident parents in your group are sharing suggestions rather than telling other parents what to do; but equally, ensure that the discussion doesn't turn into making excuses for one another. If a father is not making time to show and share the gospel with his children, then he needs challenging gently, rather than excusing.

⊻

• **If your group are mainly or all non-parents, simply ask: How can we as church members support parents in doing their God-given job?**

10. What should motivate our hard work as employees (v 5-8)?

• We are to obey our bosses as slaves of Christ (v 6), who served us as our slave by dying for us, and still serves us as our advocate before the Father. We are prepared to serve others in our work as part of doing, "the will of God" from our hearts. Whatever our work is, we can and should do it as part of our worship of our Lord.

• We are "serving the Lord, not people" (v 7). Since the whole earth belongs to the living God who provides our daily needs, when we contribute to the farming business or IT company we work for, in a small way we are helping to govern God's creation.

- "The Lord will reward each one for whatever good they do" (v 8). Even though an earthly master may not notice or care what we do, or may be biased or miserly in how they reward us, our Lord sees everything including the motives for doing it, and will delight to reward us in heaven. Christ will generously reward good works done for him, with a bonus in heaven among "the incomparable riches of his grace" (2 v 7).

What should we not allow to motivate us (v 5-8)?
- Personal advancement (v 6)
- A boss/colleague watching us, so that we work hard when we can impress someone and not when there is no one to see (v 6)

11. What do bosses need to remember (v 9)? They have a Master, too. They are accountable to God, just as their employees are. And God doesn't show any favouritism. He will not reward bosses more in heaven because of their better education or expensive clothes. CEOs and street-sweepers will stand in the same dock on judgment day, and will be praised not for their position or status but for their good works.

- **How would this shape their treatment of those working under their authority?**
- They will treat them in the way they would like to be treated.
- They will not threaten their employees with unjust or arbitrary consequences; they will not intimidate them nor take advantage of their power over them.
- They will still lead. They will use their authority well and wisely and for the good

of everyone, not just them—but they will still use it.

EXPLORE MORE
Read Mark 10 v 42-45. How does Jesus explain the difference between how the world uses authority, and how members of his kingdom use their authority?
"Gentile" rulers "lord it over" those under their authority. So they use power for their own good, to meet their own desires. But the Ruler of the church, the Son of Man who has infinite, eternal authority (see Daniel 7 v 13-14) used his power to serve, rather than to demand the service he deserves. He gave his life for those he has authority over. And when it comes to Christians who have a position of leadership, the Son of Man says we are not to follow the world—"not so with you"'—but rather the model of the serving Son of Man.

12. APPLY: How has Paul shown us we can, as Christians, display God's triumph in saving and changing his people from Monday to Saturday? The triumphant victory of the cross over evil powers is not only demonstrated in church on Sundays. It is powerfully displayed when Christians from every background submit to the rule of Christ in our homes and workplaces from Monday to Saturday as well—whether that is in leading sacrificially when we are called to, and/or in submitting when we are called to. It is wonderful to realise that in our marriages, families and workplaces, we can be pleasing Christ as we serve Christ, often in very mundane, unnoticed ways.

- **Discuss ways in which you can support each other in these three relationships—marriage, parenting/ being parented, and the workplace. Try to be specific and practical.**

8 Ephesians 6 v 10-24
SPIRITUAL WARFARE

THE BIG IDEA
The Christian life is one of standing firm against spiritual attack by "wearing" our gospel convictions as we fearlessly proclaim Christ's victory to those around us.

SUMMARY
In this final section, Paul reaches his dramatic finale to the letter: "Finally, be strong in the Lord and in his mighty power. Put on the full armour of God, so that you can take your stand against the devil's schemes" (v 10-11).

He begins "Finally" because, far from being a random diversion or disconnected afterthought, this passage is actually the glorious climax to Ephesians—and it is all about spiritual warfare. Paul outlines God's battle-plan for our spiritual resistance to the devil's scheming. He locates our unlimited supplies in God; he analyses the threat of the enemy forces to divide and conquer us; he clarifies our response in standing firm; he trains us in wearing the protective armour we will need; and then he explains his strategy for victory… namely, praying for world mission.

Satan wants to prevent people from being gathered into the church of Christ and demonstrating his defeat at the cross in the spiritual realms. Paul tells us to stand firm in the gospel and pray for world mission. So spiritual warfare is to put on the full armour of God worn by Christ, which is faith in the gospel, expressed in prayer for evangelism.

GUIDANCE FOR QUESTIONS
1. What do you think of when you hear the words "spiritual warfare"? Some will think of nothing! Others may mention films

such as *The Exorcist*; or cults, witchdoctors, etc. Not many of us think of the normal, everyday Christian life when we think of "spiritual warfare". You might find it useful to return to this question after Q9.

2. What does Paul tell us to do (v 10)? "Be strong" (literally, "be strengthened") in the mighty power of God.

3. How does he tell us to do it (v 11)? By putting on "the full armour of God".

4. Why do we need to do this (v 11-12)? Because we need to stand against "the devil's schemes" (v 11). Behind "flesh and blood" enemies (false teachers, persecutors, those who mock us, etc) stand spiritual enemies: "the spiritual forces of evil in the heavenly realms". So we are in a spiritual battle, in which we need to stand our ground, and we will need spiritual armour to do that.

EXPLORE MORE
Read Revelation 12 v 9, 12; John 8 v 44; 1 Peter 5 v 8. What do these verses tell us about the devil and his aims? He is active on earth, seeking to lead the whole world astray, filled with fury. He is a liar, and he seeks to "devour" Christians by convincing them not to trust Christ as their Lord and Saviour.
Read Luke 11 v 14-22; Colossians 2 v 13-15; 1 John 3 v 8. What do these verses tell us about what Jesus has done to the devil? In coming to earth, King Jesus brought God's kingdom and began to overpower and throw out Satan, because

he is more powerful than him; on the cross, he removed Satan's ability to use God's law against us—by demanding God punish lawbreakers justly—and so the spiritual forces of evil are now powerless to take us to hell; and so, in his life and death and resurrection, Jesus has destroyed the power and the work of Satan.

Read Revelation 20 v 7-10. What will one day happen to the devil? This is a complex passage! But notice that the main emphasis is that the devil will resist God till the end; but that in the end, he will be utterly defeated and then punished.

5. APPLY: It is easy to make too little of the devil (as Western society tends to do), or to make too much of him. Which do you find it tempting to do? What about your church? What are the dangers of making this mistake? Some of us are dangerously oblivious to satanic powers, because we're influenced by the rationalistic materialism of our culture. There is, however, the opposite risk of becoming dangerously obsessed with spiritual warfare and far too afraid of Satan. In London, for instance, there have been dreadful reports of children being brutally tortured by misguided churches attempting exorcisms because they don't understand how the deliverance ministry of Christ operates through the gospel. Many Christians need to understand that "the reason the Son of God appeared was to destroy the devil's work" (1 John 3 v 8).

• **What truths in the first part of this study do you most need to remember as you go about your life?** Encourage group members to share the (different) truths they need to remember, believe and apply—and encourage them to think through what difference that will make to

their perspective and actions.

6. What does victory in this spiritual warfare look like (v 13-14)? "Stand … stand firm." The battleground will be everyday life—the devil will try to stir up doubts in our minds and divisions in our churches, by undermining our confidence in the mystery of the gospel that unites us. Our goal is to survive, to hold our ground, standing firm together in gospel convictions.

7. Look at the armour we are to "put on" in v 14-17. It is not a list of actions. So what unites the pieces of kit that Paul identifies? When we look carefully at these pieces of armour, we soon realise that truth, righteousness, peace, faith, salvation and the word of God are not virtuous actions we are to start doing! Paul is not urging us to be good. Rather, they are all ways of describing the impact of the gospel. The full armour of God, which our champion and commander, Jesus, wore into battle with Satan, is simply faith in the gospel, which the devil wants us to abandon.

8. What does it look like to "wear" this armour? Think about how each piece of armour helps us with the various attacks—lies—of the devil. This reinforces the truth that to "wear" the armour God provides is simply to remember, believe and live by the truths of the gospel. So when the devil attacks us by suggesting that God is not good, or not trustworthy, or that his word is not clear, it is a gospel conviction that will protect us and enable us to stand firm by resisting the temptation to listen to the devil's lies and sin in some way. So work through each item of armour and think about what lie/temptation it helps a Christian to resist, eg: when I am tempted to doubt that something is sinful just because the Bible says it is, I need to "wear" the belt of truth and use the sword of the Spirit; when tempted to keep quiet about the gospel, I need to put on the "sandals" of gospel-readiness (v 15). Of course, the armour's items overlap, and it is not the case that each temptation has one piece of armour that resists it. We need to wear *all* these gospel convictions.

9. What final piece of "armour" does Paul identify in verse 18? Prayer. Notice that this prayer is regular ("on all occasions"); varied ("all kinds"—whether urgent, single-sentence prayers, family prayers at the start or end of the day, or longer prayers in church, or prolonged prayer at times of pressure or decision); persistent ("keep on"); and for other believers, not just ourselves ("for all the Lord's people"). **Why is it so powerful (look back to 1 v 19b-22; 3 v 20-21)?** Because the power we ask for from God as we pray is the same power that raised Jesus from his tomb; and it is therefore able to do more than we could ever think to ask.

• **Why is Paul asking for this kind of prayer (v 19-20)? Why is he particularly in need of prayer for this, given his situation?** He asks for courage in evangelism, twice asking for prayer to preach "fearlessly". As he explains "the mystery of the gospel"—that Jews and Gentiles alike can and must be saved through faith in Christ crucified—it brings him persecution, and he is currently imprisoned. Wearing God's armour may also mean wearing chains in prison. So it is tempting for him to be fearful, and fear would keep his mouth closed. So he requests prayer for fearlessness so that he will speak the gospel "as I should".

⌄

• **Is our attitude towards evangelism the same as Paul's?** Do we accept that preaching the gospel faithfully will sometimes lead to rejection or persecution? Do we love the Lord enough to proclaim the gospel even so? Do we ask for prayer? Do we accept that we "should" proclaim the gospel?

10. Paul uses three words in his final farewell that sum up what we've seen about God throughout the letter. How are these three words great summaries?

• **Peace (v 23):** This is the wonderful reconciliation with God and with each other for which Christ died, by which we are gathered together under Christ in his church. Indeed Christ "is our peace"—the one in whom we are united because he died, "thus making peace" by satisfying God for our sins, so that "he came and preached peace" (2 v 14-17). Peace well summarises the eternal blessing of salvation in Christ that results from the mystery of the gospel.

• **Love (v 23):** God's eternal plan does not only reveal how impressive God is, but how compassionate he is; not just how powerful he is, but how loving. Paul has already celebrated how immense this love for us is (3 v 18). Love well summarises the substance of what we experience in Christ through faith in the mystery of the gospel.

• **Grace (v 24):** Grace is undeserved and extravagant kindness, and it is the origin of God's plan not only to gather us into his church to display his wisdom in the spiritual realms, but "in order that in the coming ages he might show the incomparable riches of his grace, expressed in his kindness to us in Christ Jesus" (2 v 7). Grace is the origin of the mystery of the gospel now revealed in Christ to all who continue to love him with "an undying love" (6 v 24). Since our salvation comes entirely from his grace, all glory must be given entirely and eternally to him.

11. APPLY: In what way is your praying for the gospel to be preached part of God's great plan for the world? We have seen throughout Ephesians that God's great plan is to gather redeemed people into unity under Christ, for eternity. When we pray for world mission—and for our own witness closer to home—we are part of his great plan, and we are resisting Satan's temptation to keep the gospel to ourselves, or to fail to believe that it will ever have an impact. .

• **How can you encourage each other to pray for others as verses 18-19 lay out, as a group and as a church?** Members of your group might want to meet to pray together for those who are engaged in mission, and for each other; your church prayer meeting could perhaps include a regular time for praying for evangelism, local and international; etc.
You might like to encourage each group member to share one person for whom they would like the group to be praying, and that they would faithfully, fearlessly tell them the gospel this week.

12. APPLY: How has God's triumphant plan, revealed in Ephesians, to gather everything under the risen Christ as displayed in his churches shaped your view of:
• **the purpose of your local church?**
• **your safety from Satan's attacks?**
• **the glory of evangelism?**

This is an opportunity to think back over the whole letter, and identify and share personal "highlights", based on the great themes of Ephesians. Give your group a few minutes to flick through the letter and write down some notes before you share together.

OPTIONAL EXTRA
Either before or after Q12, read through the whole letter together, either in one go or allowing your group to "interrupt" in order to praise God for what they have just heard.

EPHESIANS FOR YOU

The latest in this ground-breaking series, Richard brings his careful Bible-handling and clear insights to this wonderful book. Written for Christians of every age and stage, whether new believers or pastors and teachers, each title in the series takes a detailed look at a part of the Bible in a readable, relevant way.

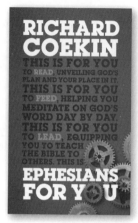

Ephesians For You is for you:

- **to read**, mapping out the themes, promises and challenges of the epistle

- **to feed,** using it as a daily devotional, complete with helpful reflection questions

- **to lead,** equipping small-group leaders and Bible teachers and preachers to explain, illustrate and apply this wonderful book of the Bible.

Find out more at:
www.thegoodbook.co.uk/for-you

UK & Europe: www.thegoodbook.co.uk
Australia: www.thegoodbook.com.au
North America: www.thegoodbook.com
New Zealand: www.thegoodbook.co.nz

UK & Europe: 0333 123 0880
Australia: (02) 6100 4211
North America: 866 244 2165
New Zealand (+64) 3 343 1990